GUITAR PRACTICE PLANNER

CUSTOMIZABLE WEEKLY ORGANIZER FOR TEACHERS AND STUDENTS

CONTENTS

Alfred Music
P.O. Box 10003
Van Nuys, CA 91410-0003
alfred.com

ISBN-10: 1-4706-3380-9 (Book)
ISBN-13: 978-1-4706-3380-6 (Book)

Cover Photos
Classical guitar by Richard Bruné.
Fender Stratocaster courtesy of Fender Musical Instruments, Inc.
Martin D-16 acoustic courtesy of Martin Guitar Company.

ABOUT PRACTICING

There are many talented guitarists in the world but *great* players are rare. Often, the difference between a talented player and a great one is the quality of their practice, so thoughtful practice, and dedication to it, can make all the difference.

Making the Most of Your Practice Time

Practice involves learning through experimentation and building skills through repetition. Experimentation—or developing your imagination—is very important, and the type of experimentation you do depends on the style of guitar you're learning. A rock guitarist's goals will differ from a classical guitarist's, but both will need to train their hands to play well. Using practice time wisely is essential to making lasting improvements.

Tips for Good Practice

The ingredients for good practice may vary depending on what you're working on, but the following tips for good practice apply to many situations.

Slow and steady wins the race. Doing things quickly won't necessarily get you to your goal sooner, so try practicing at a pace that allows you to be in complete control. This way, you won't make mistakes, get tense, or feel stressed. Whatever you repeat will become habit, so try not to repeat mistakes. Instead, take your time, avoid repeating mistakes, and work on developing good habits. This will help build confidence.

Less is more. Practice small sections at a time. For example, take just two measures of the music you're working on and practice them until you can play those measures smoothly and accurately. This method will be much easier to accomplish than trying to take on an entire piece all at once. Learn two measures, then two more, followed by two more, and so on.

Failing to plan is planning to fail. To play well, you must practice well. Always have clear goals for your practice time. Make very specific plans. For example, if you are practicing how to change from a C chord to a G chord, make a plan for every step it takes to get that done. Know the exact finger movements, or transitions, needed. When you practice a chord change slowly, you'll master it quickly!

Look before you leap. Look at your music before you try to play it, and make sure you are mentally ready to start. Here are some things to look for before playing.

- Do you know the names of all the notes?

- Have you thought about what fingers are going to be used and how they are going to move?

- Are you comfortable with the rhythms in the music?

- Are there repeats, dynamics, articulation marks such as accents or staccato, or any other notation markings that will affect how you play the music?

Working with a Teacher

Having a good teacher is very helpful. They provide essential information about music and guitar technique that will guide your practice and allow you to learn more quickly and easily. What you're practicing will depend on your level and the style of music you're studying. If you're an advanced player, you may be playing full songs or advanced pieces. If you're a beginner, you will probably be working through a well-paced beginning method book. In either case, a good teacher will help you *structure your practice time,* which is where this practice planner comes in.

About the Practice Planner

For Both Guitar Teachers and Students

This planner will help both guitar teachers and students. Teachers can use this planner to help organize their student's course of study. If a teacher writes down all of the assignments at each lesson, they'll have a complete, detailed log of their lessons. Whether working with a teacher or on your own, this planner will help keep track of what you're practicing and let you see the progress you have made—which is an encouraging reminder of how much you have improved.

How to Use the Practice Planner

Everybody practices in different ways, and the flexibility of this planner will let you use it in the way that is most effective for you.

- At the top of the page there's a space to write the date of the lesson. Right next to it, there's a space for writing the page numbers assigned from your method book. In the subject column on the far left, underneath the date, the teacher can indicate up to seven different practice subjects, including four lines to write in descriptions and goals. The subjects should include everything being worked on at that lesson or during that week. A suggested number of minutes to devote to the subject can be included.

- Use the *BPM* (beats per minute) column to keep track of your development. Consistently noting the BPM will help you track how your speed increases from week to week.

- The calendar on the right provides fields for each day of the week. You, and/or your teacher, should customize the calendar to make the lessons and practice time as effective as possible. You may choose to simply put a check under the **M** when you finish practicing a subject on Monday, or you can write in the number of minutes spent on each subject that day.

- At the bottom of the calendar, there's room to include notes about the practice week or assignments. This can be an important record, since you can review your practice planner's previous weeks, or months, and reflect on the progress you have made.

Use the right-hand page, which includes blank music manuscript and blank chord and scale frames, to write out additional lesson material, such as scales, chords, licks, or anything else that isn't included in your method book or songbook.

USING THIS PRACTICE PLANNER

Assigned pages.

Date of the lesson.

The BPM (beats per minute) column keeps track of your speed development.

Current practice subjects.

Description of the practice subject, and/or student's current goals.

Amount of daily time student should spend working on practice subject.

When the student finishes practicing a subject, they can check off the practice session under the corresponding day of the week or write in the actual number of minutes spent on the subject that day.

Teacher's observations, additional helpful reminders, tips, etc.

Student's observations about his/her practice week, assignments, etc.

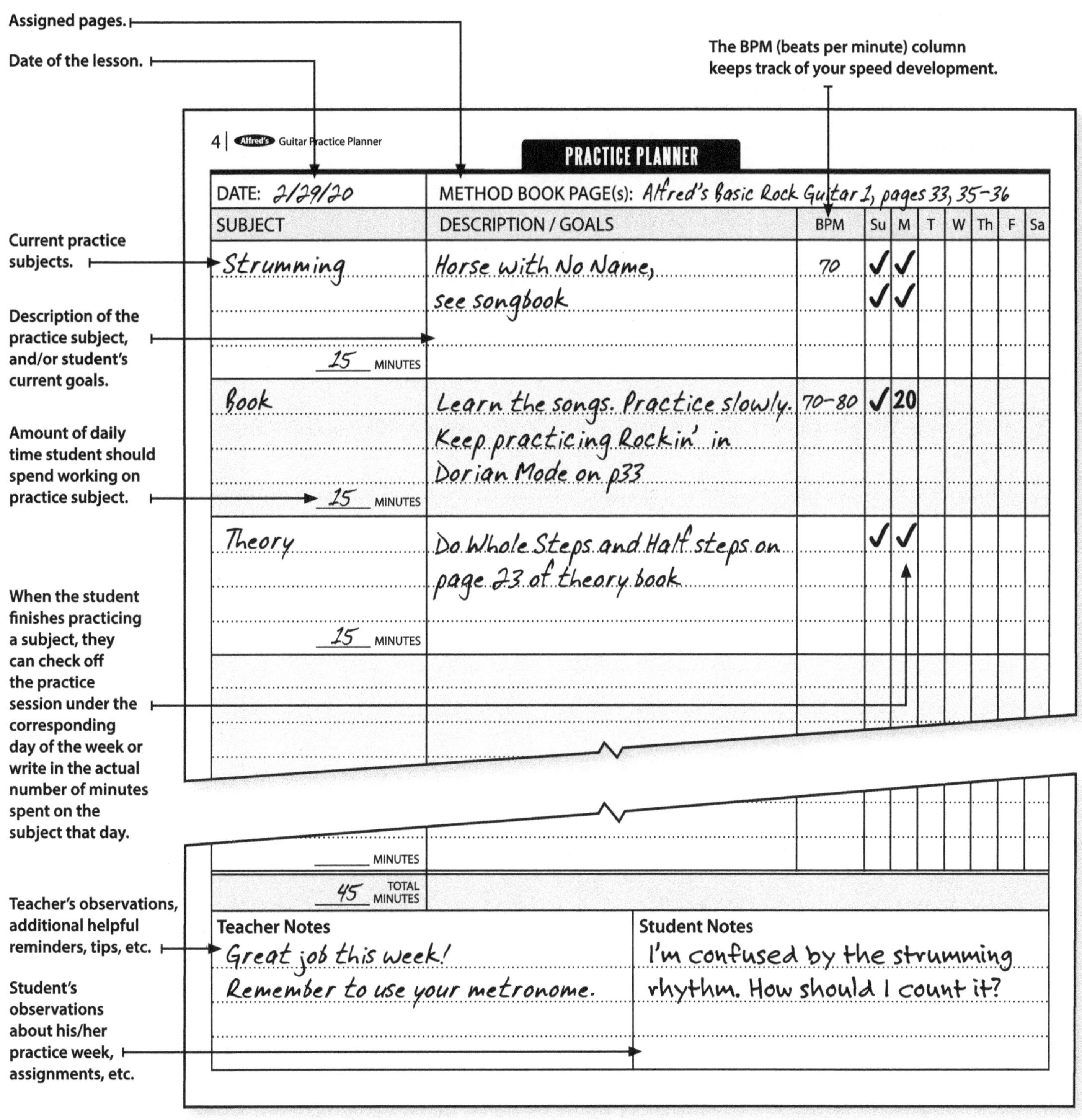

Look over the previous weeks or months entered in your practice planner to see the progress you've made.

PRACTICE PLANNER

DATE:	METHOD BOOK PAGE(s):								
SUBJECT	DESCRIPTION / GOALS	BPM	Su	M	T	W	Th	F	Sa
________ MINUTES									
________ MINUTES									
________ MINUTES									
________ MINUTES									
________ MINUTES									
________ MINUTES									
________ MINUTES									
TOTAL ________ MINUTES									

Teacher Notes

Student Notes

PRACTICE PLANNER

DATE:	METHOD BOOK PAGE(s):								
SUBJECT	**DESCRIPTION / GOALS**	BPM	Su	M	T	W	Th	F	Sa
__________ MINUTES									
__________ MINUTES									
__________ MINUTES									
__________ MINUTES									
__________ MINUTES									
__________ MINUTES									
__________ MINUTES									
TOTAL __________ MINUTES									

Teacher Notes

Student Notes

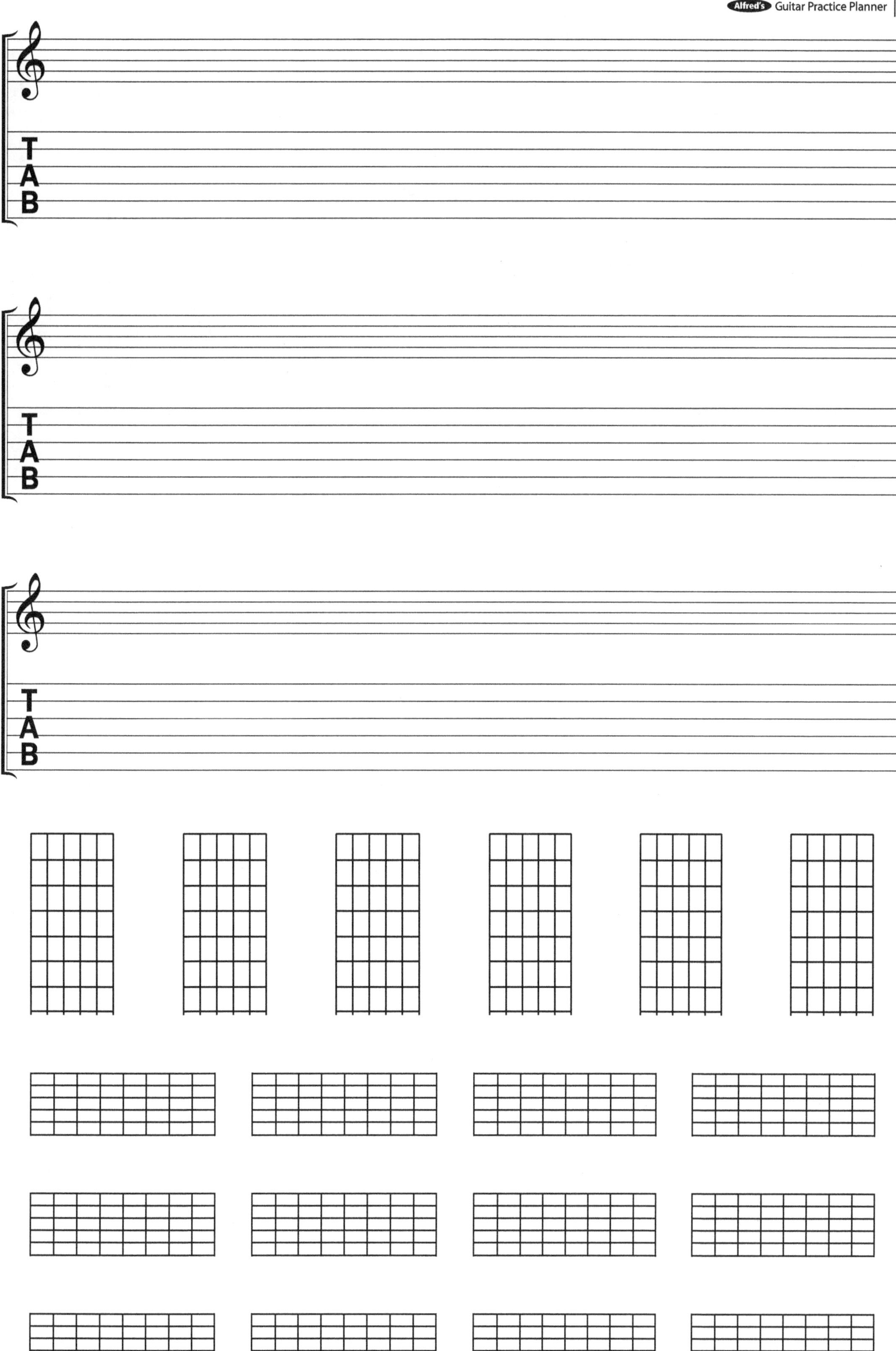

PRACTICE PLANNER

DATE:	METHOD BOOK PAGE(s):								
SUBJECT	DESCRIPTION / GOALS	BPM	Su	M	T	W	Th	F	Sa
_______ MINUTES									
_______ MINUTES									
_______ MINUTES									
_______ MINUTES									
_______ MINUTES									
_______ MINUTES									
_______ MINUTES									
TOTAL _______ MINUTES									

Teacher Notes

Student Notes

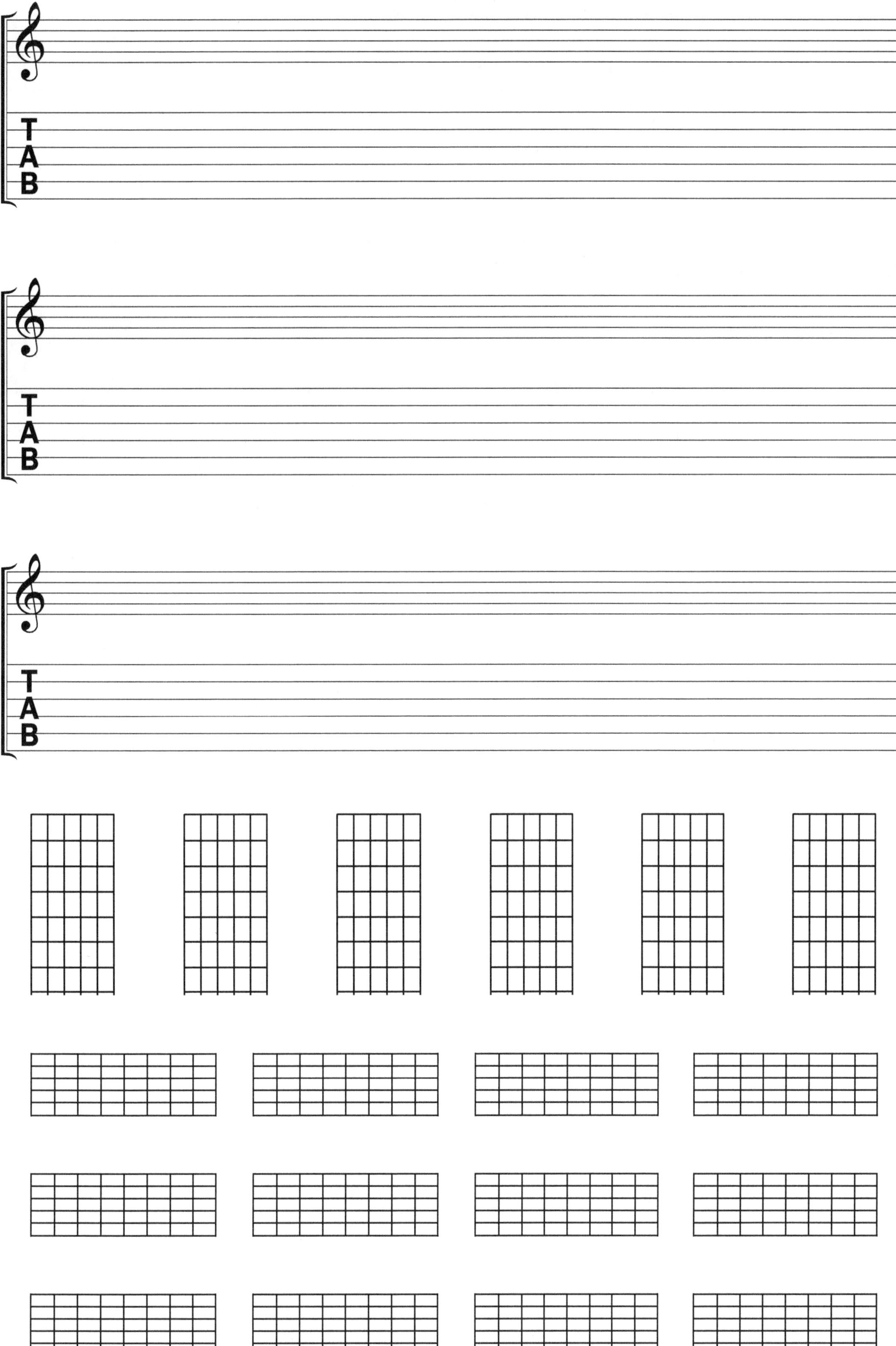

PRACTICE PLANNER

DATE:	METHOD BOOK PAGE(s):								
SUBJECT	**DESCRIPTION / GOALS**	BPM	Su	M	T	W	Th	F	Sa
_______ MINUTES									
_______ MINUTES									
_______ MINUTES									
_______ MINUTES									
_______ MINUTES									
_______ MINUTES									
_______ MINUTES									
_______ TOTAL MINUTES									

Teacher Notes

Student Notes

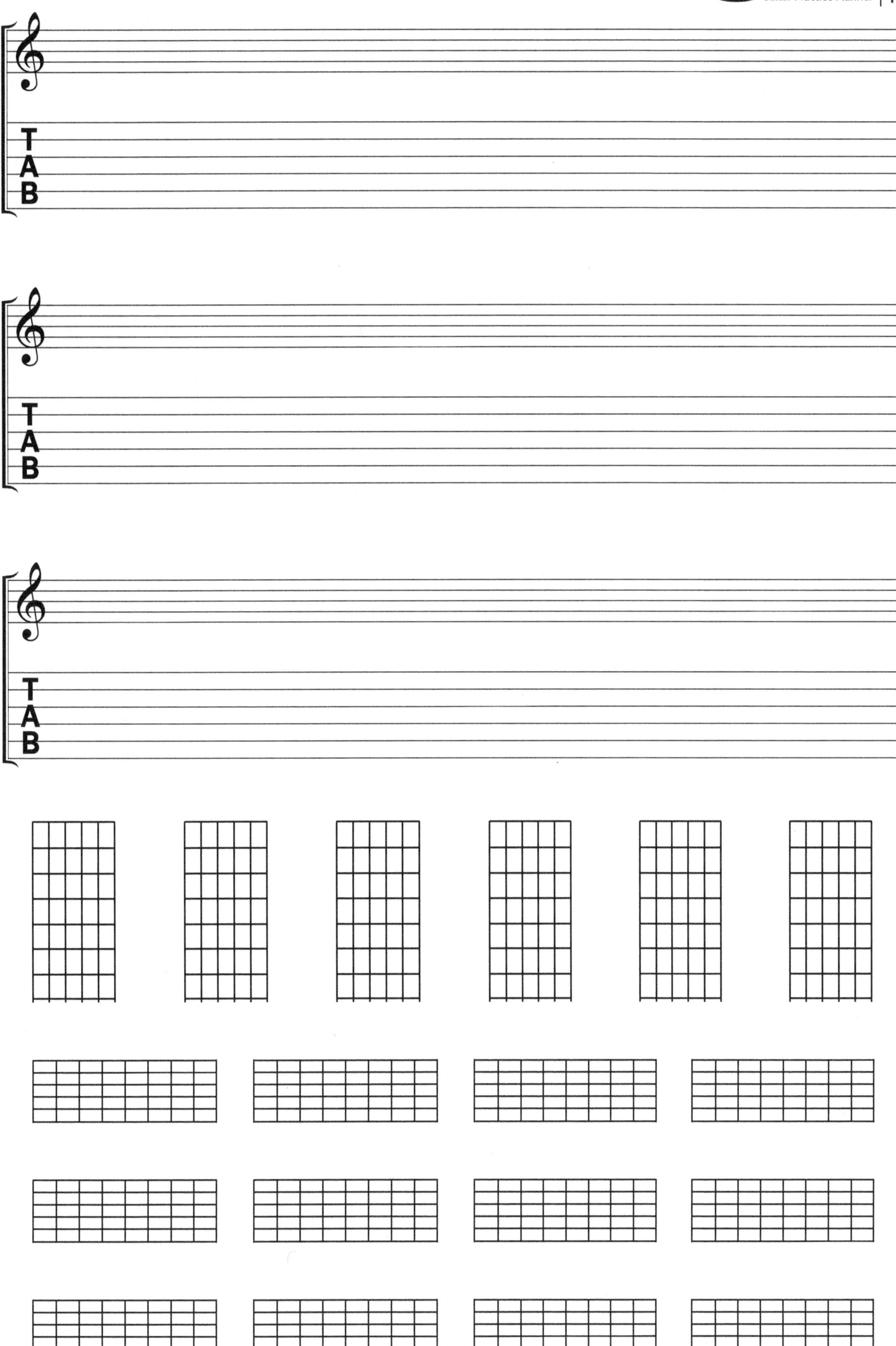

PRACTICE PLANNER

DATE:	METHOD BOOK PAGE(s):								
SUBJECT	**DESCRIPTION / GOALS**	BPM	Su	M	T	W	Th	F	Sa
________ MINUTES									
________ MINUTES									
________ MINUTES									
________ MINUTES									
________ MINUTES									
________ MINUTES									
________ MINUTES									
TOTAL ________ MINUTES									

Teacher Notes

Student Notes

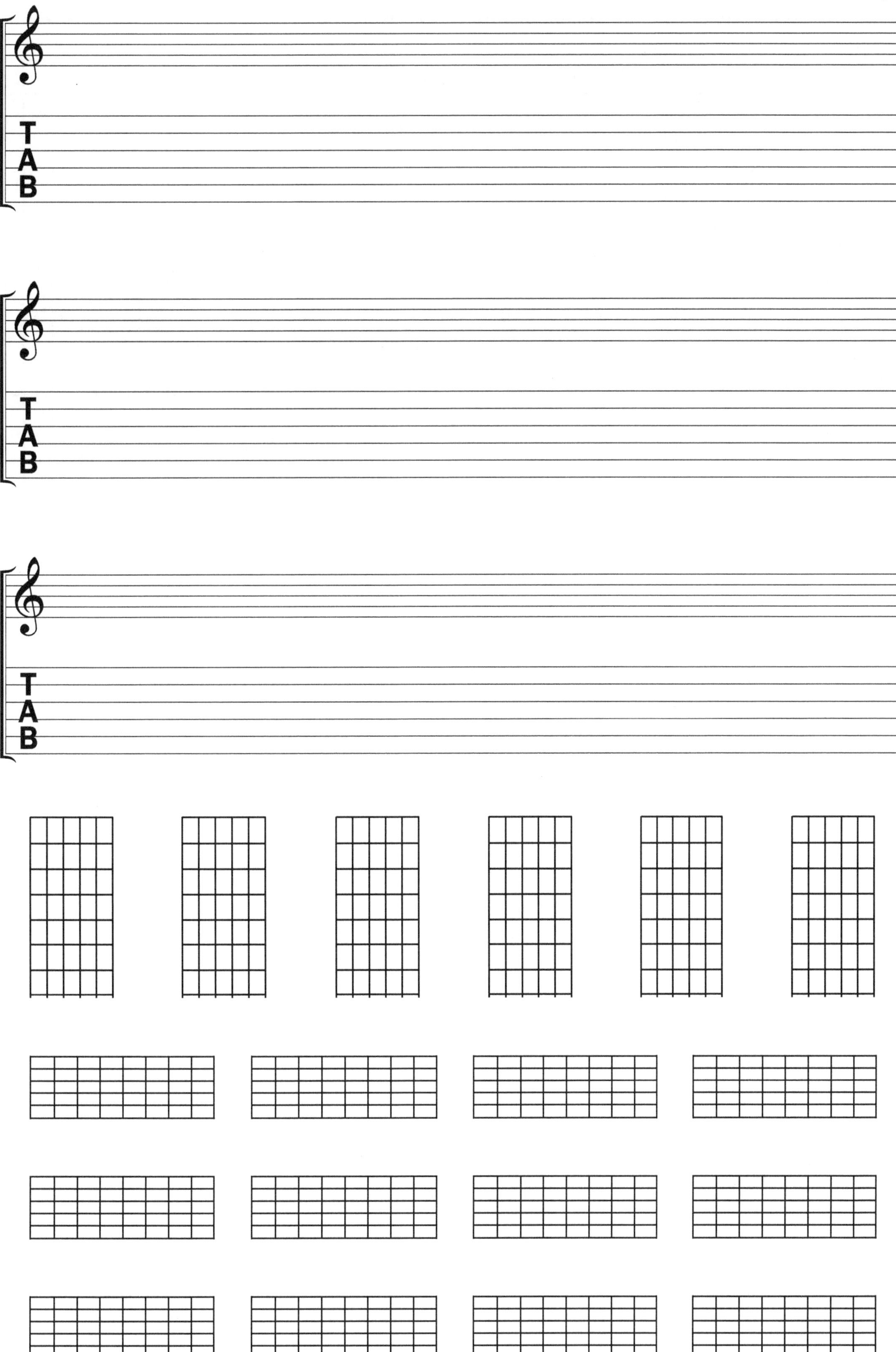

PRACTICE PLANNER

DATE:	METHOD BOOK PAGE(s):									
SUBJECT	DESCRIPTION / GOALS	BPM	Su	M	T	W	Th	F	Sa
__________ MINUTES									
__________ MINUTES									
__________ MINUTES									
__________ MINUTES									
__________ MINUTES									
__________ MINUTES									
__________ MINUTES									
TOTAL __________ MINUTES									

Teacher Notes

Student Notes

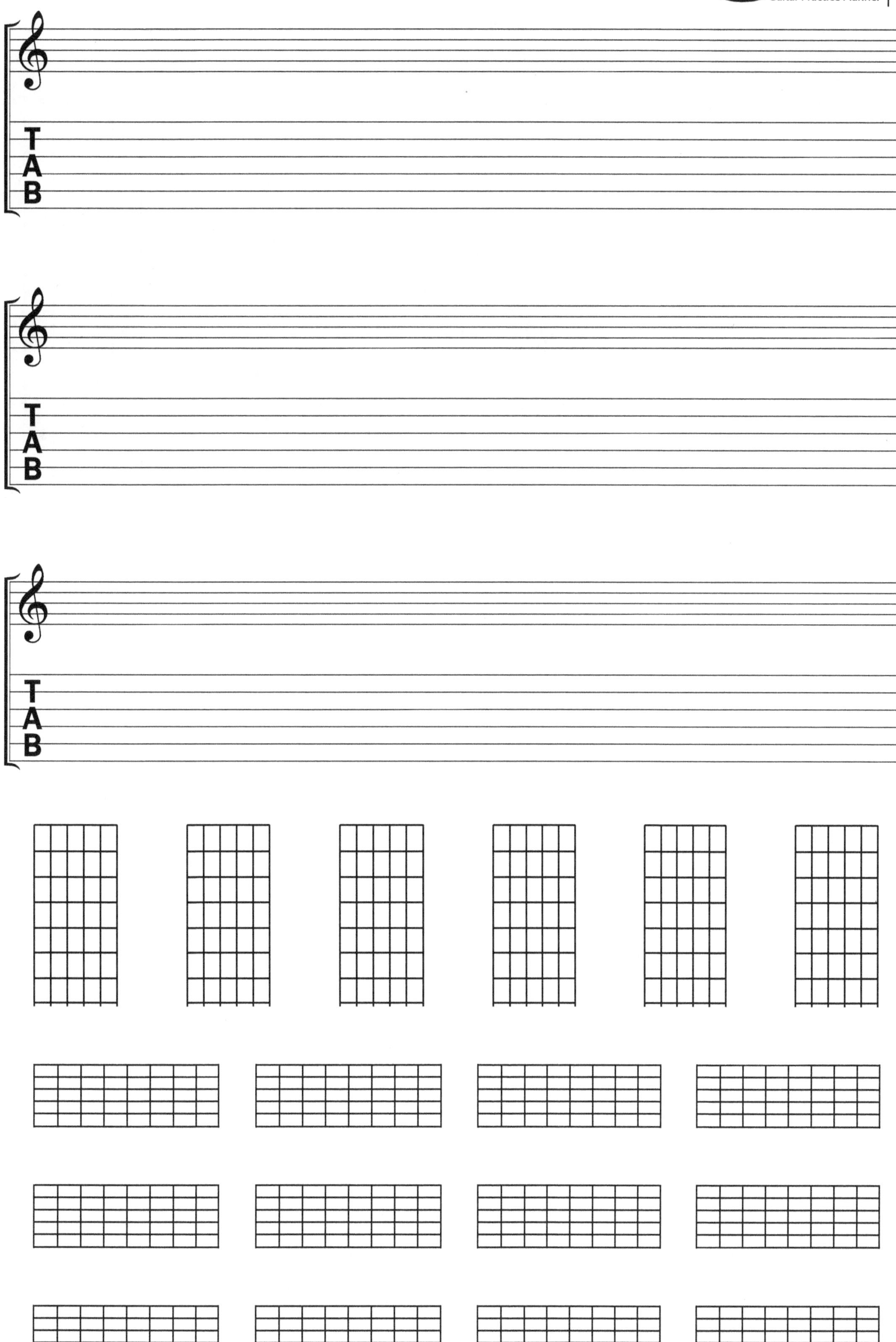

PRACTICE PLANNER

DATE:	METHOD BOOK PAGE(s):									
SUBJECT	**DESCRIPTION / GOALS**	**BPM**	Su	M	T	W	Th	F	Sa
________ MINUTES									
________ MINUTES									
________ MINUTES									
________ MINUTES									
________ MINUTES									
________ MINUTES									
________ MINUTES									
TOTAL ________ MINUTES									

Teacher Notes

Student Notes

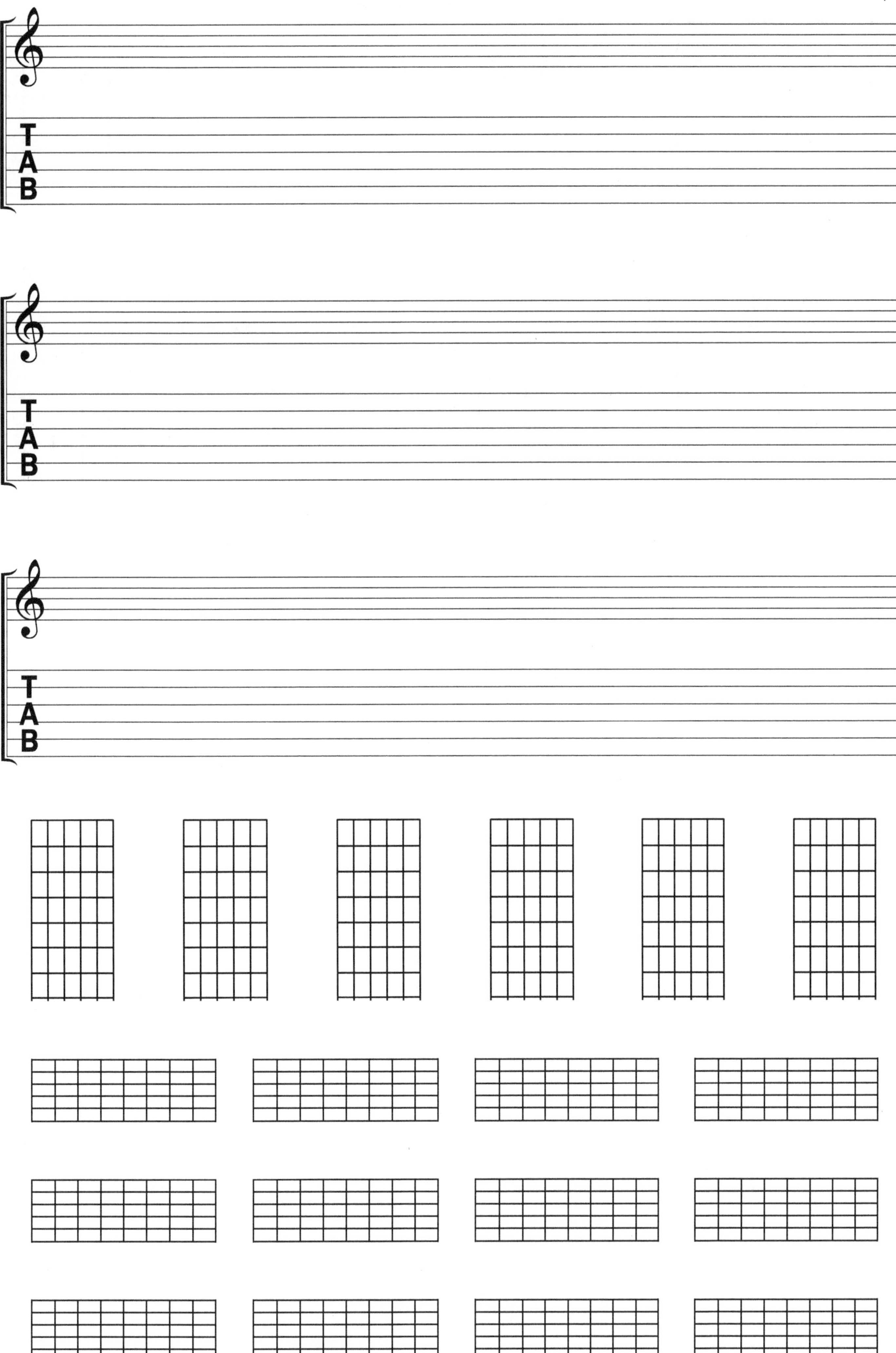

PRACTICE PLANNER

DATE:	METHOD BOOK PAGE(s):									
SUBJECT	DESCRIPTION / GOALS	BPM	Su	M	T	W	Th	F	Sa
__________ MINUTES									
__________ MINUTES									
__________ MINUTES									
__________ MINUTES									
__________ MINUTES									
__________ MINUTES									
__________ MINUTES									
TOTAL __________ MINUTES									

Teacher Notes

Student Notes

PRACTICE PLANNER

DATE:	METHOD BOOK PAGE(s):									
SUBJECT	DESCRIPTION / GOALS	BPM	Su	M	T	W	Th	F	Sa
_______ MINUTES									
_______ MINUTES									
_______ MINUTES									
_______ MINUTES									
_______ MINUTES									
_______ MINUTES									
_______ MINUTES									
TOTAL _______ MINUTES									

Teacher Notes

Student Notes

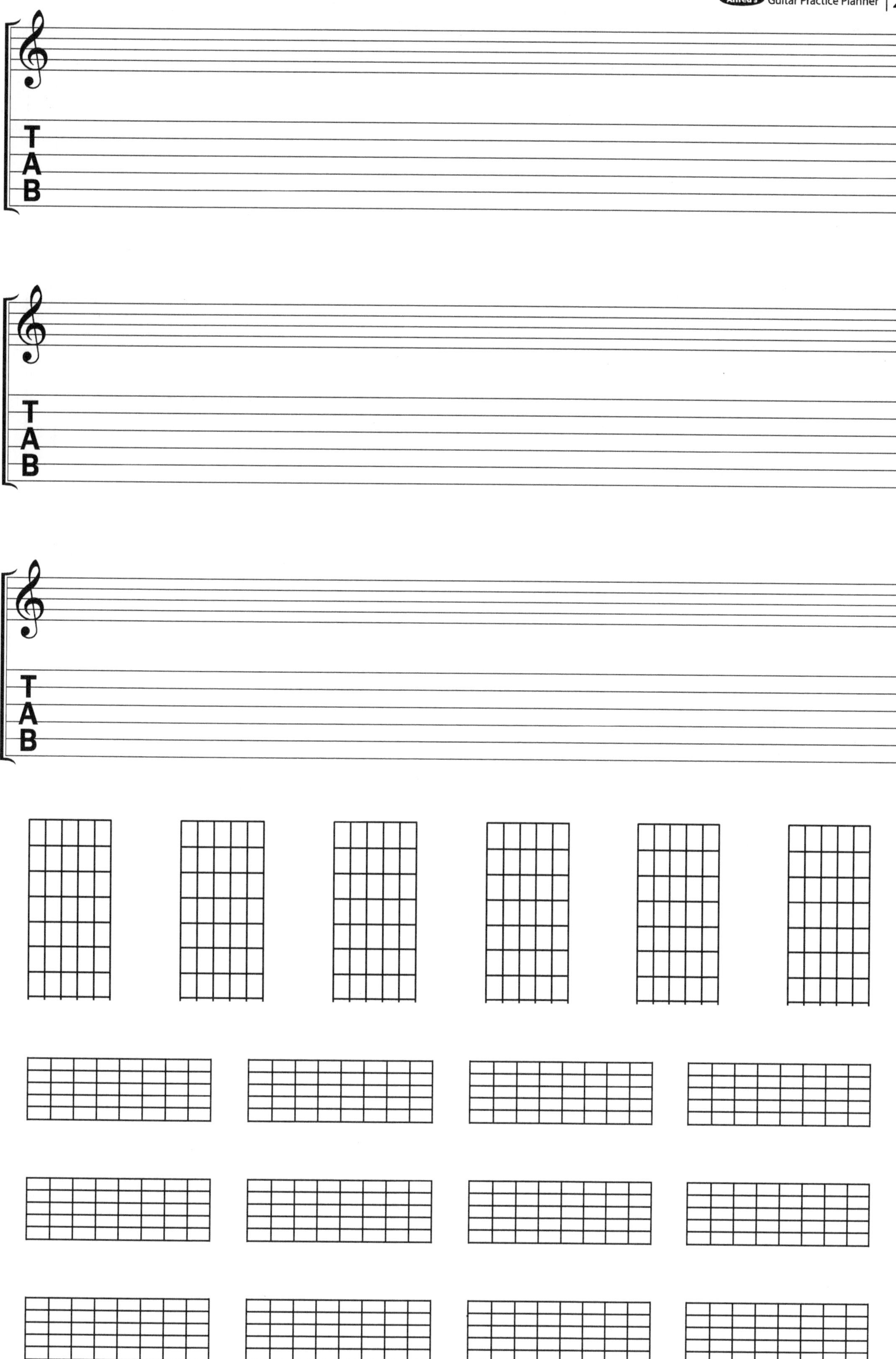

PRACTICE PLANNER

DATE:	METHOD BOOK PAGE(s):									
SUBJECT	**DESCRIPTION / GOALS**	**BPM**	**Su**	**M**	**T**	**W**	**Th**	**F**	**Sa**	
______ MINUTES										
______ MINUTES										
______ MINUTES										
______ MINUTES										
______ MINUTES										
______ MINUTES										
______ MINUTES										
TOTAL ______ **MINUTES**										

Teacher Notes

Student Notes

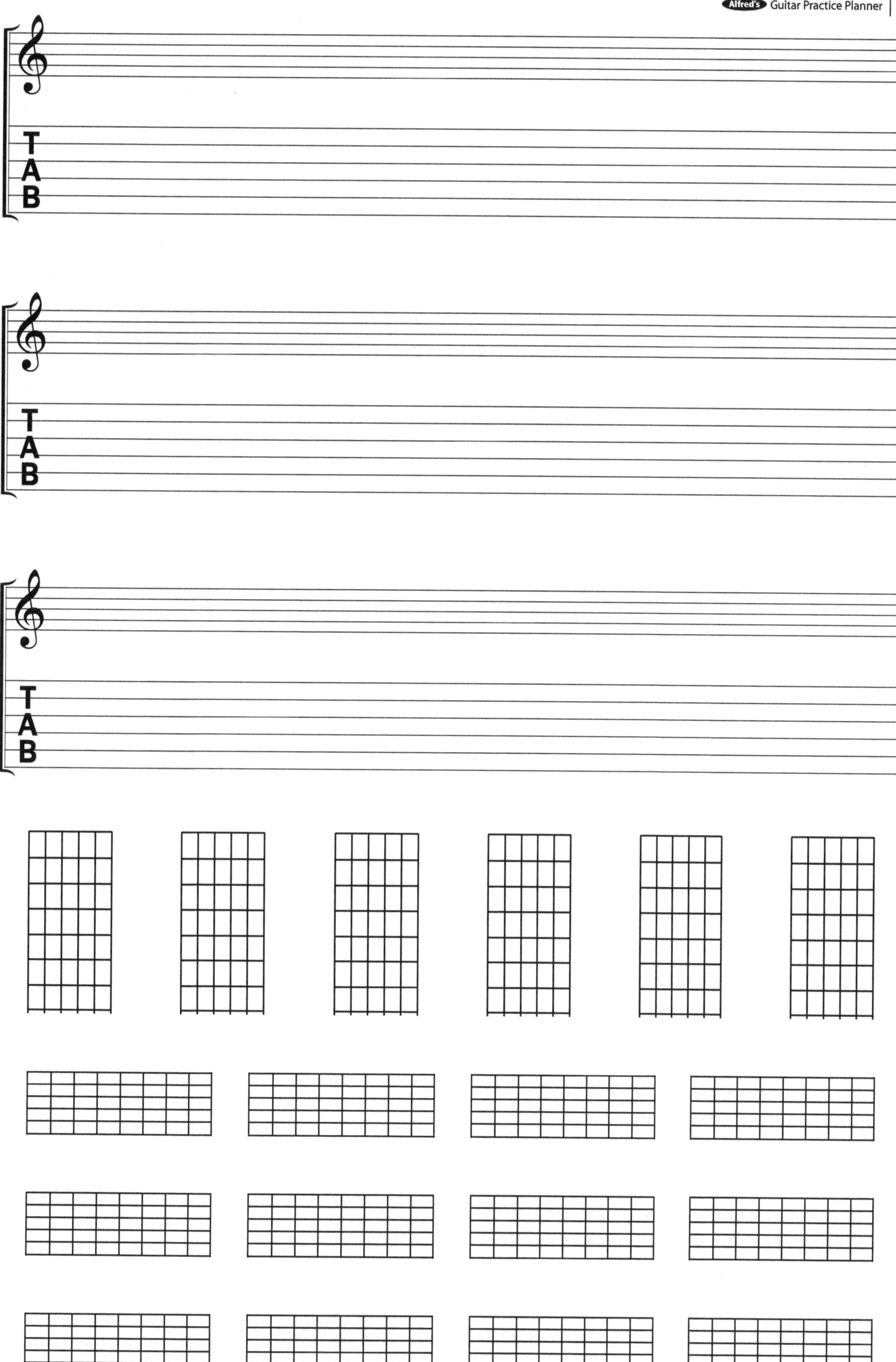

PRACTICE PLANNER

DATE:	METHOD BOOK PAGE(s):									
SUBJECT	**DESCRIPTION / GOALS**	**BPM**	**Su**	**M**	**T**	**W**	**Th**	**F**	**Sa**	
_______ MINUTES										
_______ MINUTES										
_______ MINUTES										
_______ MINUTES										
_______ MINUTES										
_______ MINUTES										
_______ MINUTES										
_______ TOTAL MINUTES										

Teacher Notes

Student Notes

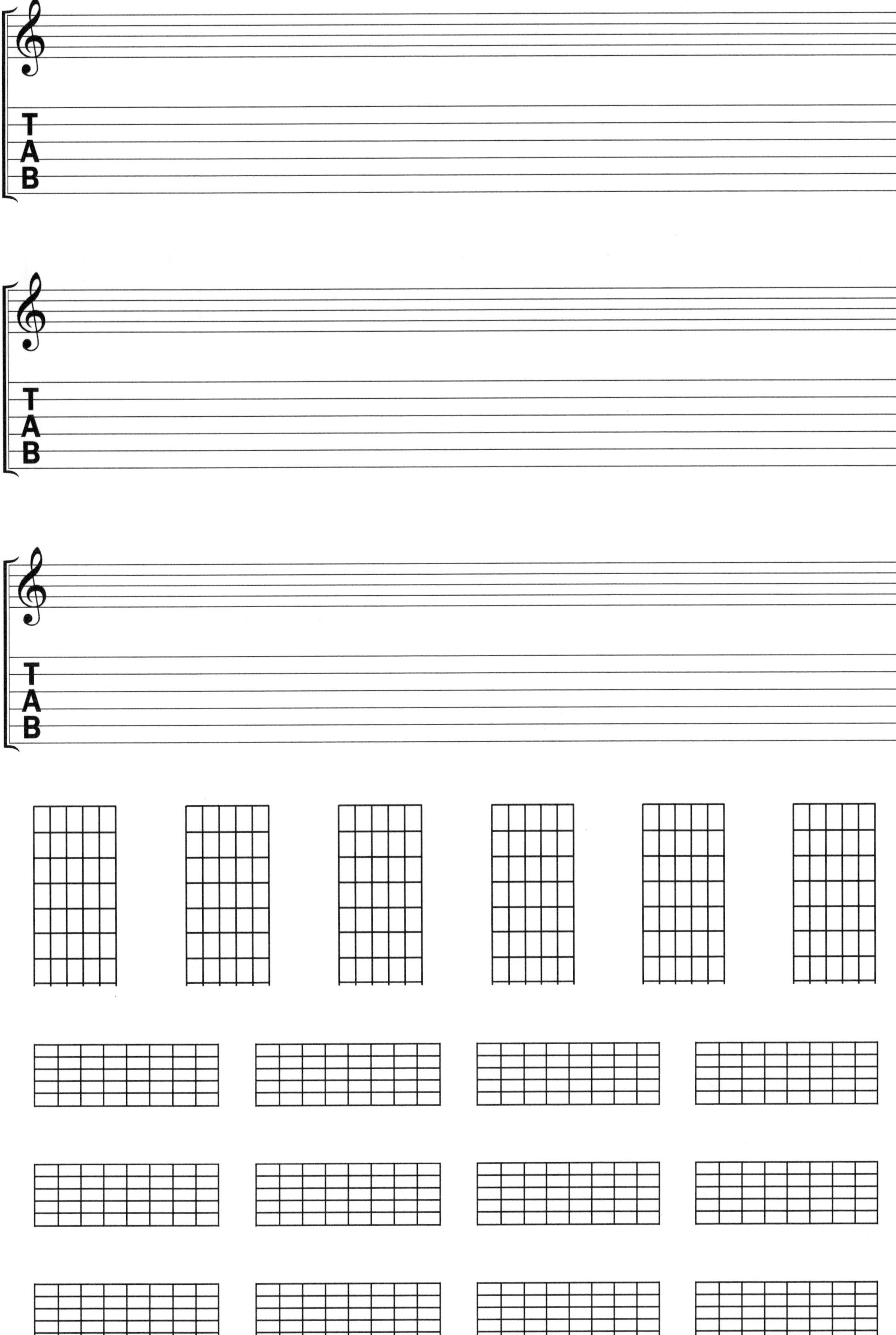

PRACTICE PLANNER

DATE:	METHOD BOOK PAGE(s):									
SUBJECT	**DESCRIPTION / GOALS**	**BPM**	**Su**	**M**	**T**	**W**	**Th**	**F**	**Sa**	
________ MINUTES										
________ MINUTES										
________ MINUTES										
________ MINUTES										
________ MINUTES										
________ MINUTES										
________ MINUTES										
TOTAL MINUTES ________										

Teacher Notes

Student Notes

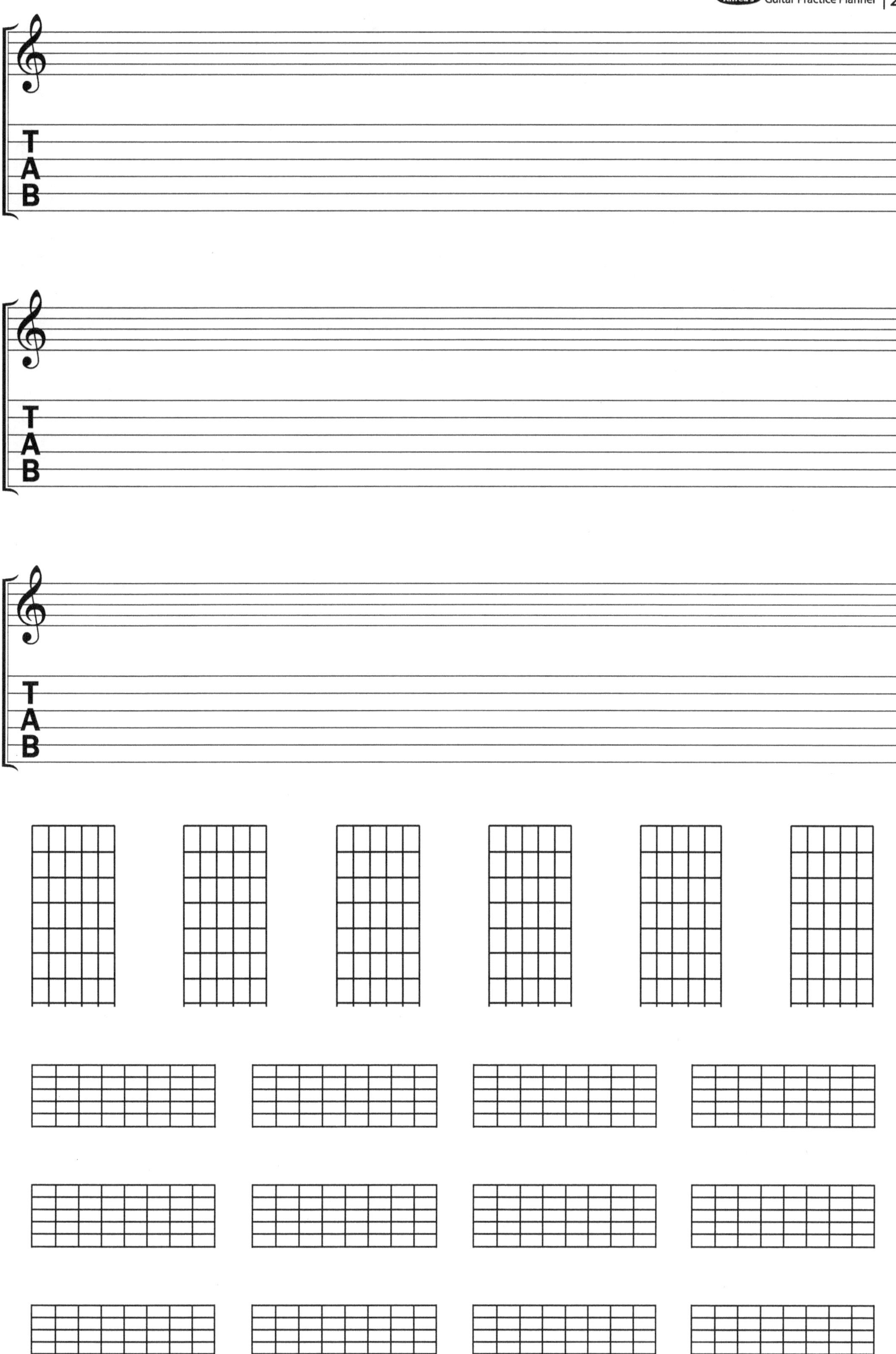

PRACTICE PLANNER

DATE:	METHOD BOOK PAGE(s):									
SUBJECT	DESCRIPTION / GOALS	BPM	Su	M	T	W	Th	F	Sa
________ MINUTES									
________ MINUTES									
________ MINUTES									
________ MINUTES									
________ MINUTES									
________ MINUTES									
________ MINUTES									
TOTAL ________ MINUTES									

Teacher Notes

Student Notes

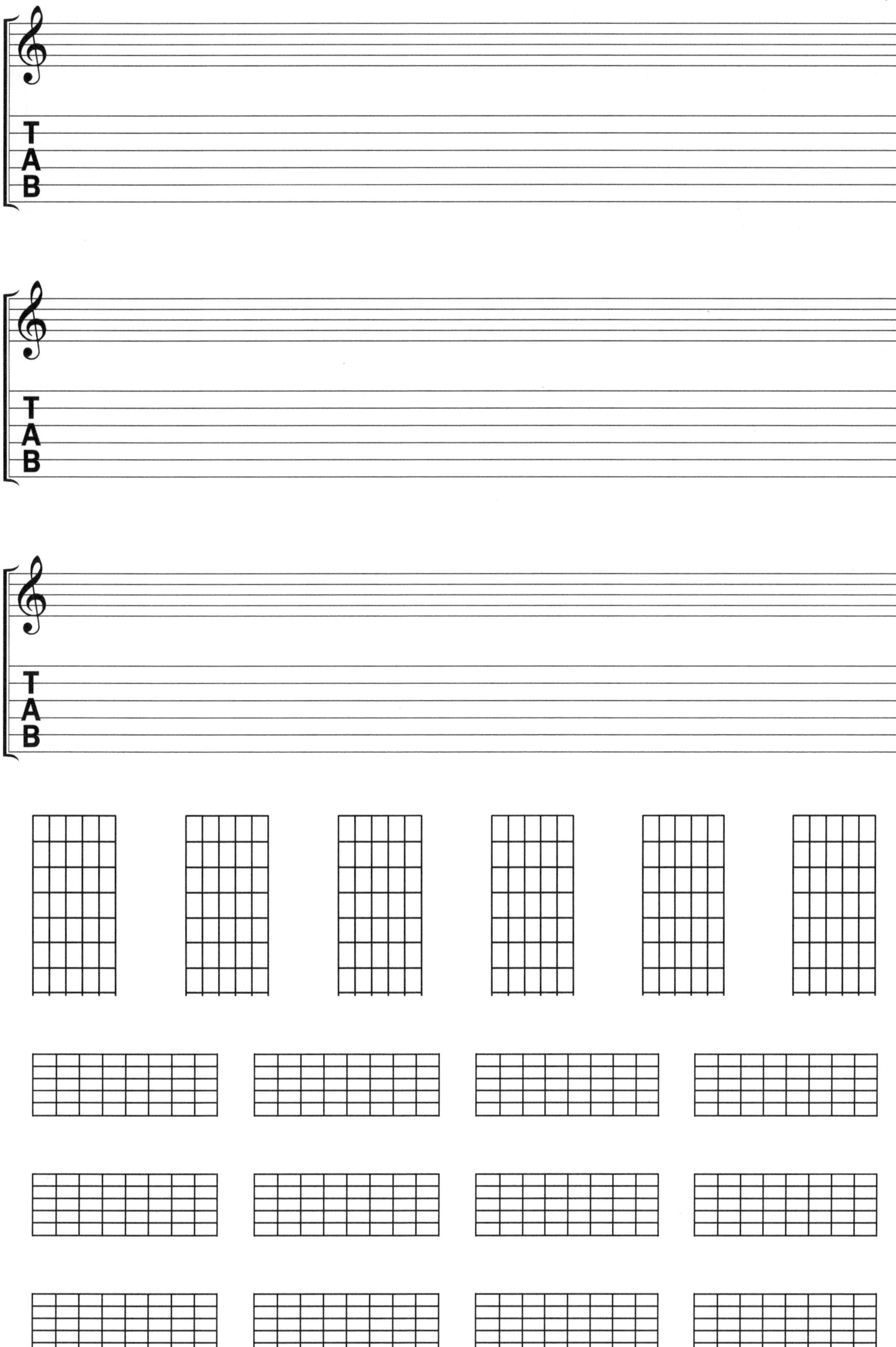

PRACTICE PLANNER

DATE:	METHOD BOOK PAGE(s):									
SUBJECT	DESCRIPTION / GOALS	BPM	Su	M	T	W	Th	F	Sa
__________ MINUTES									
__________ MINUTES									
__________ MINUTES									
__________ MINUTES									
__________ MINUTES									
__________ MINUTES									
__________ MINUTES									
TOTAL __________ MINUTES									

Teacher Notes

Student Notes

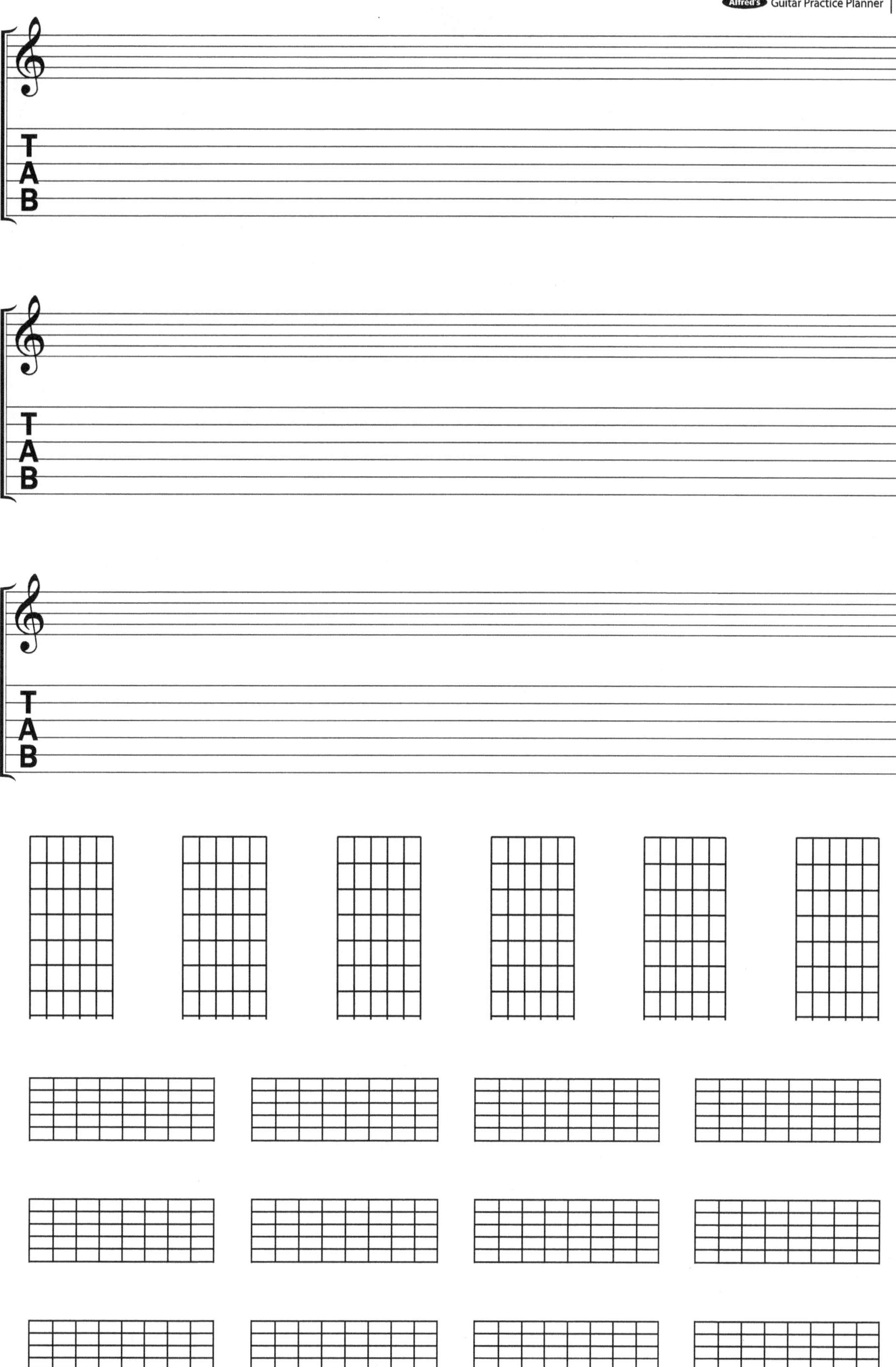

PRACTICE PLANNER

DATE:	METHOD BOOK PAGE(s):								
SUBJECT	DESCRIPTION / GOALS	BPM	Su	M	T	W	Th	F	Sa
_______ MINUTES									
_______ MINUTES									
_______ MINUTES									
_______ MINUTES									
_______ MINUTES									
_______ MINUTES									
_______ MINUTES									
TOTAL _______ MINUTES									

Teacher Notes

Student Notes

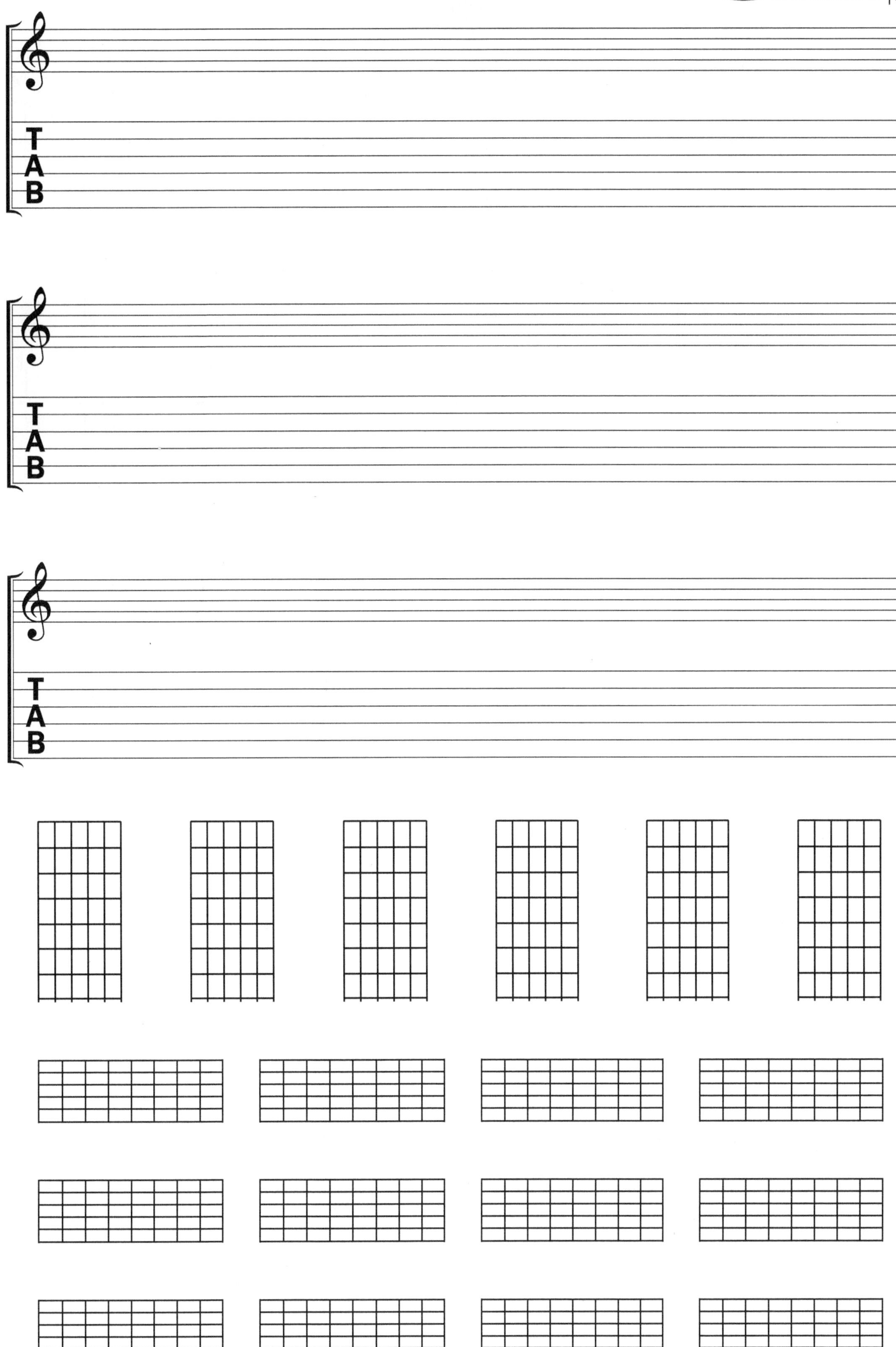

PRACTICE PLANNER

DATE:	METHOD BOOK PAGE(s):									
SUBJECT	**DESCRIPTION / GOALS**	**BPM**	**Su**	**M**	**T**	**W**	**Th**	**F**	**Sa**	
_______ MINUTES										
_______ MINUTES										
_______ MINUTES										
_______ MINUTES										
_______ MINUTES										
_______ MINUTES										
_______ MINUTES										
TOTAL MINUTES										

Teacher Notes

Student Notes

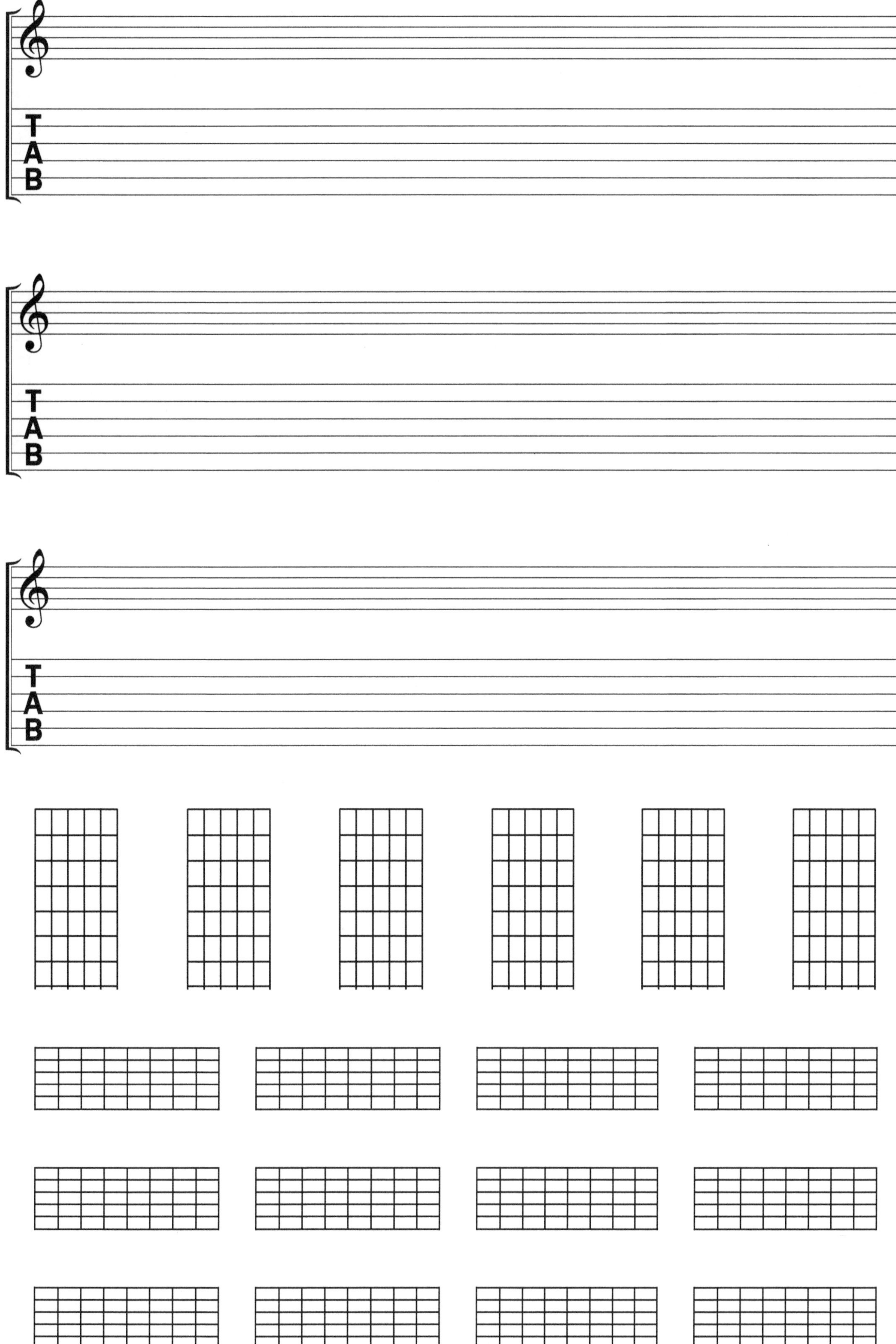

PRACTICE PLANNER

DATE:	METHOD BOOK PAGE(s):								
SUBJECT	**DESCRIPTION / GOALS**	**BPM**	**Su**	**M**	**T**	**W**	**Th**	**F**	**Sa**
__________ MINUTES									
__________ MINUTES									
__________ MINUTES									
__________ MINUTES									
__________ MINUTES									
__________ MINUTES									
__________ MINUTES									
__________ TOTAL MINUTES									

Teacher Notes

Student Notes

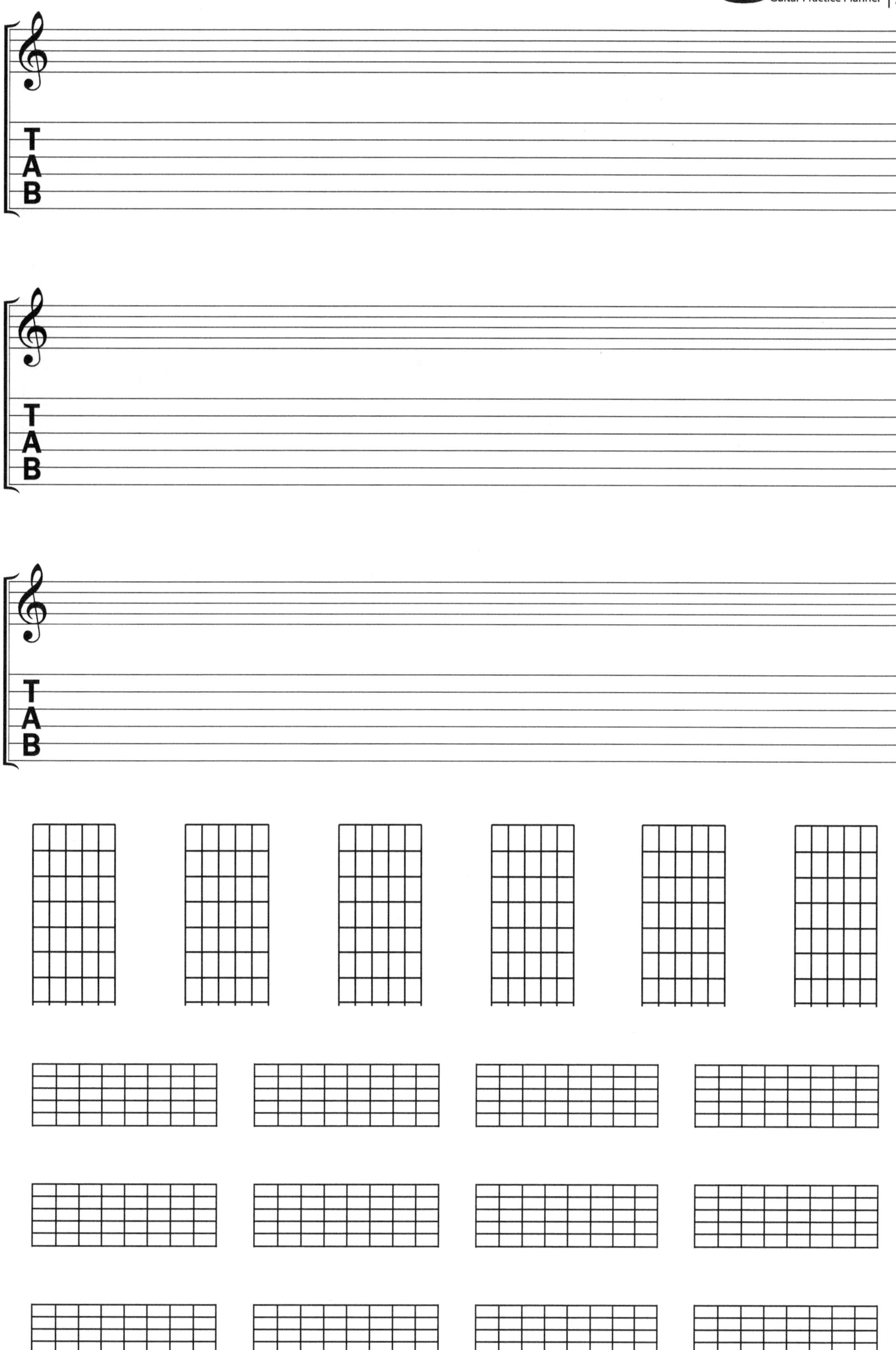

PRACTICE PLANNER

DATE:	METHOD BOOK PAGE(s):									
SUBJECT	DESCRIPTION / GOALS	BPM	Su	M	T	W	Th	F	Sa
__________ MINUTES									
__________ MINUTES									
__________ MINUTES									
__________ MINUTES									
__________ MINUTES									
__________ MINUTES									
__________ MINUTES									
TOTAL __________ MINUTES									

Teacher Notes

Student Notes

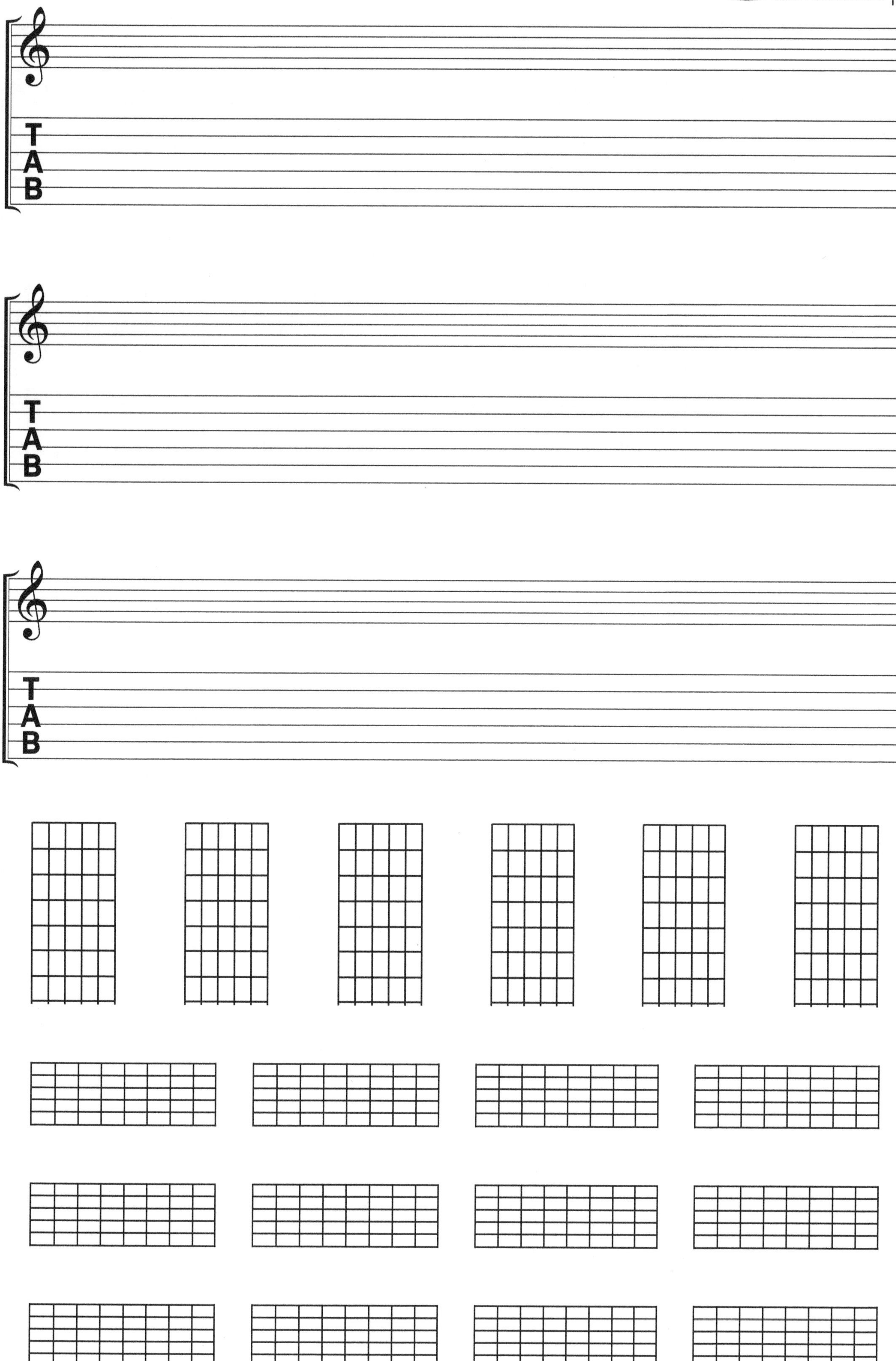

PRACTICE PLANNER

DATE:	METHOD BOOK PAGE(s):								
SUBJECT	**DESCRIPTION / GOALS**	**BPM**	**Su**	**M**	**T**	**W**	**Th**	**F**	**Sa**
_________ MINUTES									
_________ MINUTES									
_________ MINUTES									
_________ MINUTES									
_________ MINUTES									
_________ MINUTES									
_________ MINUTES									
TOTAL _________ **MINUTES**									

Teacher Notes

Student Notes

PRACTICE PLANNER

DATE:	METHOD BOOK PAGE(s):								
SUBJECT	DESCRIPTION / GOALS	BPM	Su	M	T	W	Th	F	Sa
__________ MINUTES									
__________ MINUTES									
__________ MINUTES									
__________ MINUTES									
__________ MINUTES									
__________ MINUTES									
__________ MINUTES									
TOTAL __________ MINUTES									

Teacher Notes

Student Notes

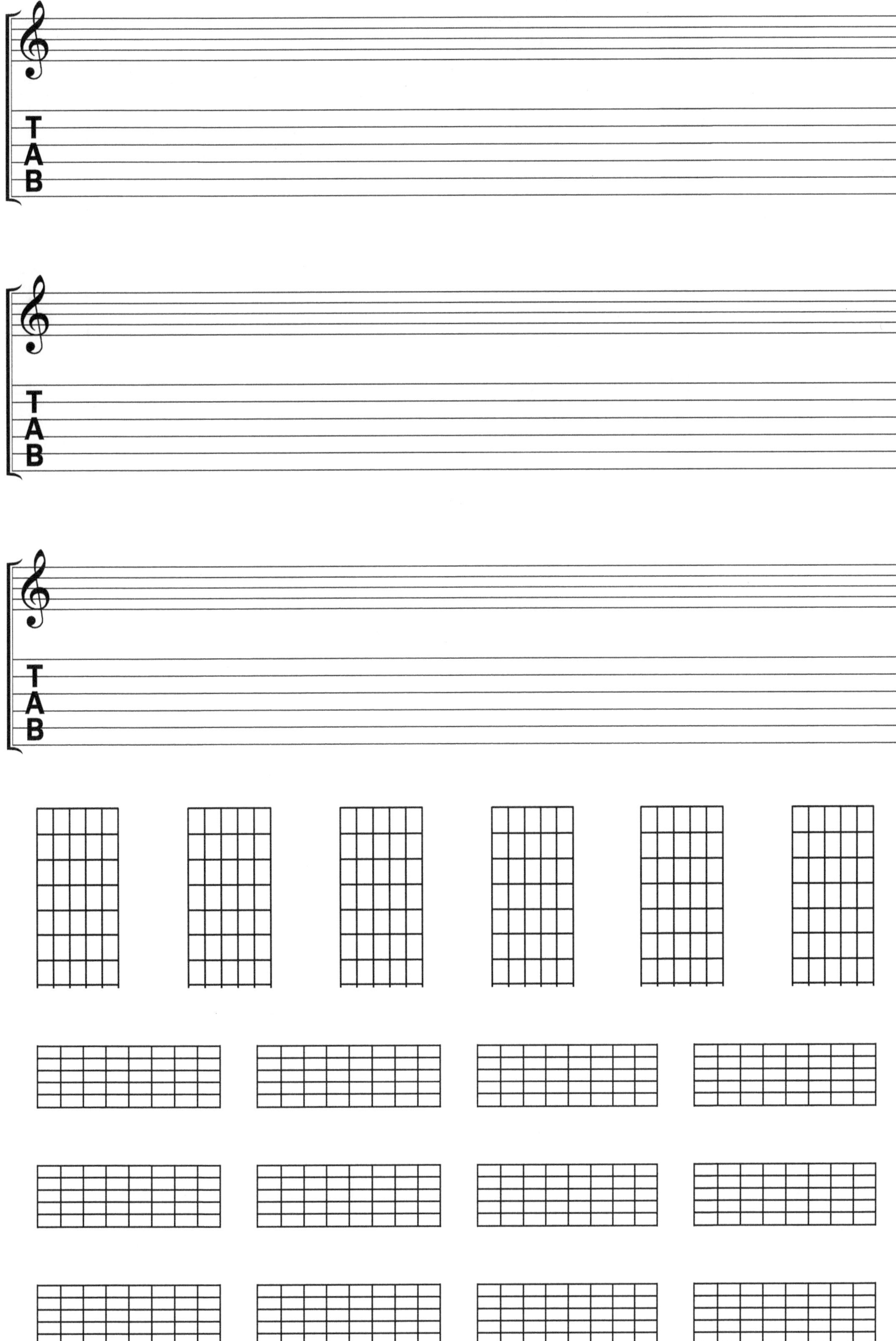

PRACTICE PLANNER

DATE:	METHOD BOOK PAGE(s):									
SUBJECT	**DESCRIPTION / GOALS**	**BPM**	**Su**	**M**	**T**	**W**	**Th**	**F**	**Sa**	
_______ MINUTES										
_______ MINUTES										
_______ MINUTES										
_______ MINUTES										
_______ MINUTES										
_______ MINUTES										
_______ MINUTES										
TOTAL _______ **MINUTES**										

Teacher Notes

Student Notes

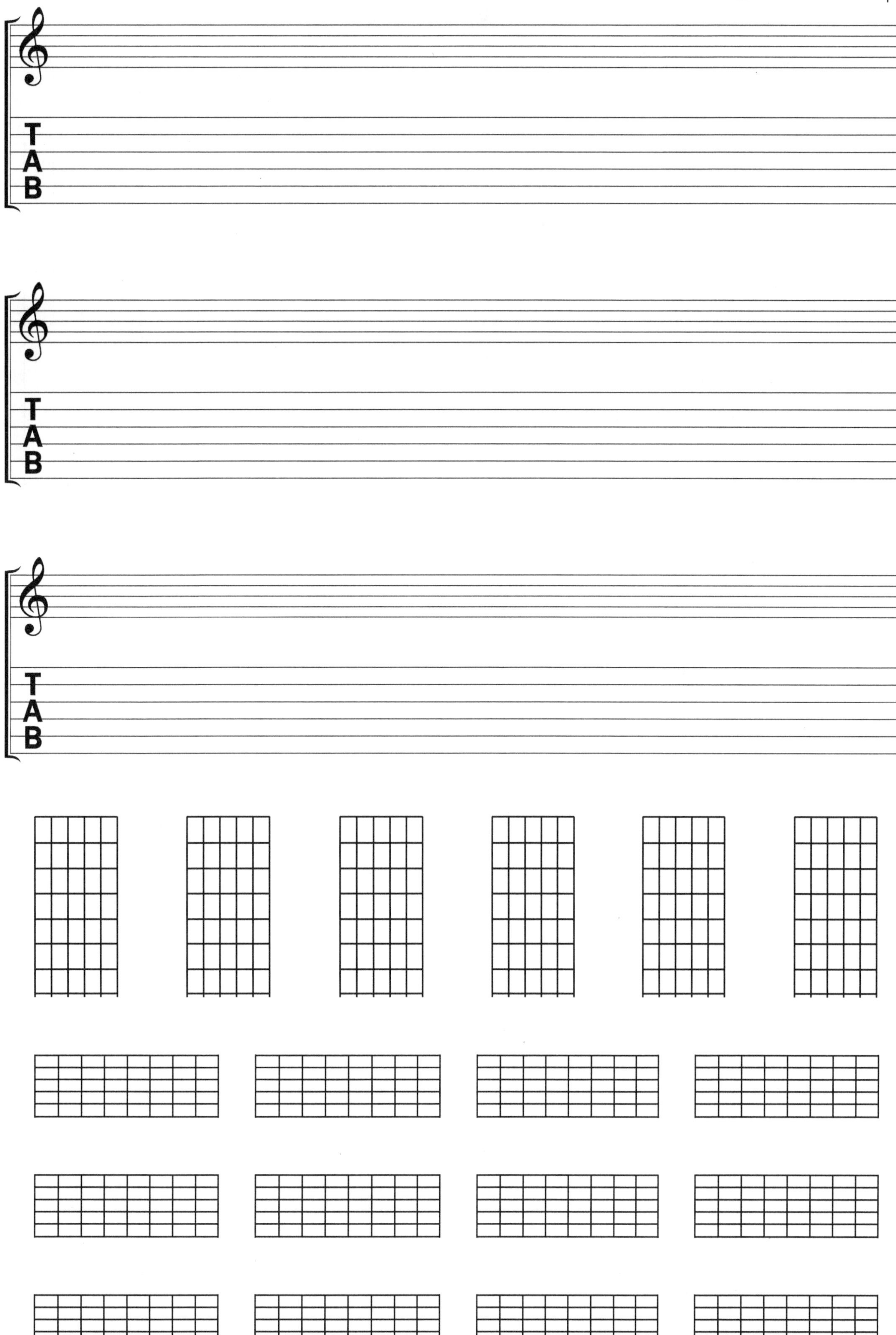

PRACTICE PLANNER

DATE:	METHOD BOOK PAGE(s):									
SUBJECT	**DESCRIPTION / GOALS**	**BPM**	**Su**	**M**	**T**	**W**	**Th**	**F**	**Sa**	
_______ MINUTES										
_______ MINUTES										
_______ MINUTES										
_______ MINUTES										
_______ MINUTES										
_______ MINUTES										
_______ MINUTES										
TOTAL _______ **MINUTES**										

Teacher Notes

Student Notes

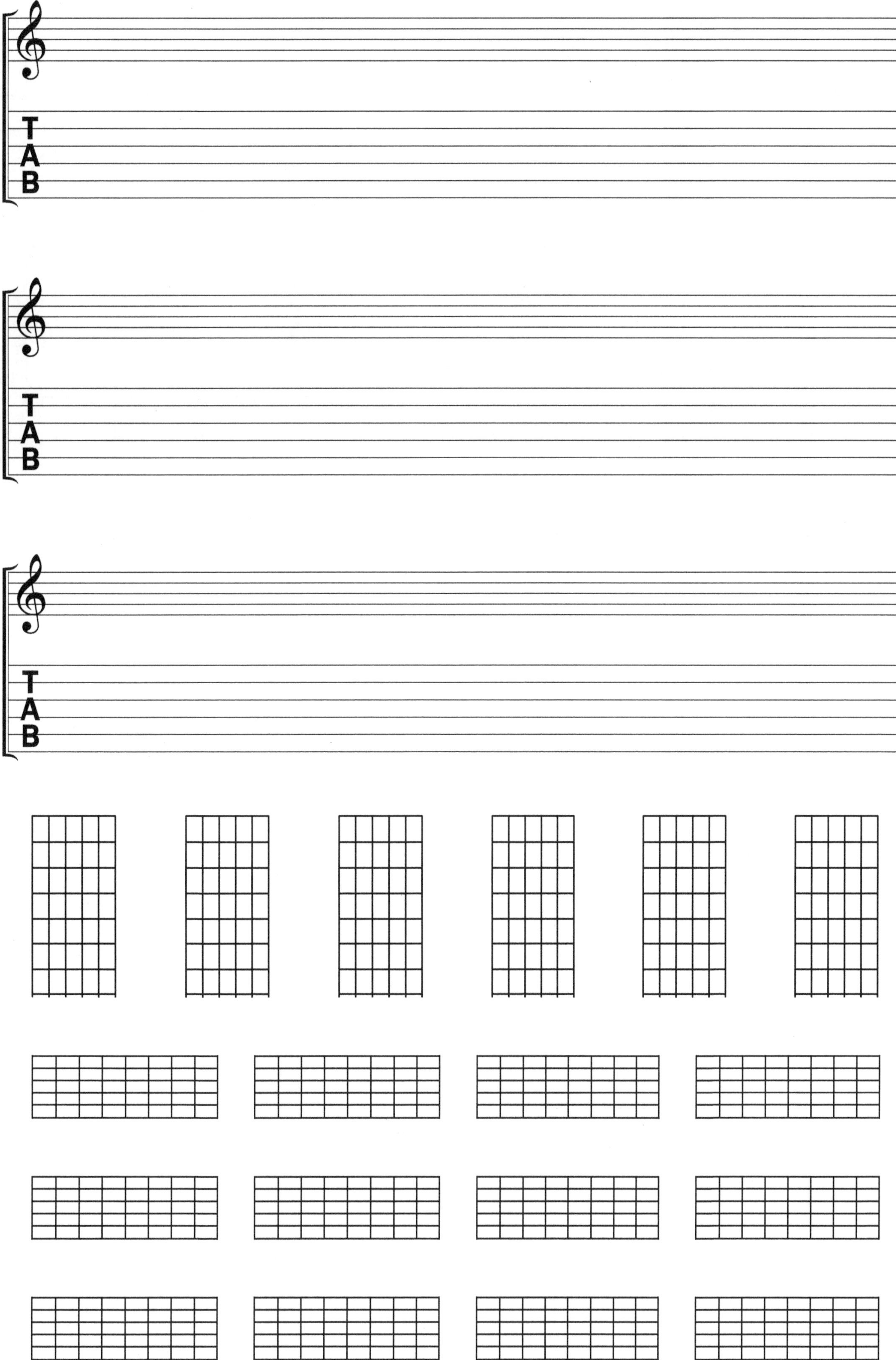

PRACTICE PLANNER

DATE:	METHOD BOOK PAGE(s):									
SUBJECT	DESCRIPTION / GOALS	BPM	Su	M	T	W	Th	F	Sa

__________ MINUTES

__________ MINUTES

__________ MINUTES

__________ MINUTES

__________ MINUTES

__________ MINUTES

__________ MINUTES

TOTAL __________ MINUTES

Teacher Notes

Student Notes

PRACTICE PLANNER

DATE:	METHOD BOOK PAGE(s):									
SUBJECT	DESCRIPTION / GOALS	BPM	Su	M	T	W	Th	F	Sa
_______ MINUTES									
_______ MINUTES									
_______ MINUTES									
_______ MINUTES									
_______ MINUTES									
_______ MINUTES									
_______ MINUTES									
TOTAL _______ MINUTES									

Teacher Notes

Student Notes

TAB

TAB

TAB

PRACTICE PLANNER

DATE:	METHOD BOOK PAGE(s):									
SUBJECT	**DESCRIPTION / GOALS**	**BPM**	**Su**	**M**	**T**	**W**	**Th**	**F**	**Sa**	
_________ MINUTES										
_________ MINUTES										
_________ MINUTES										
_________ MINUTES										
_________ MINUTES										
_________ MINUTES										
_________ MINUTES										
TOTAL MINUTES										

Teacher Notes

Student Notes

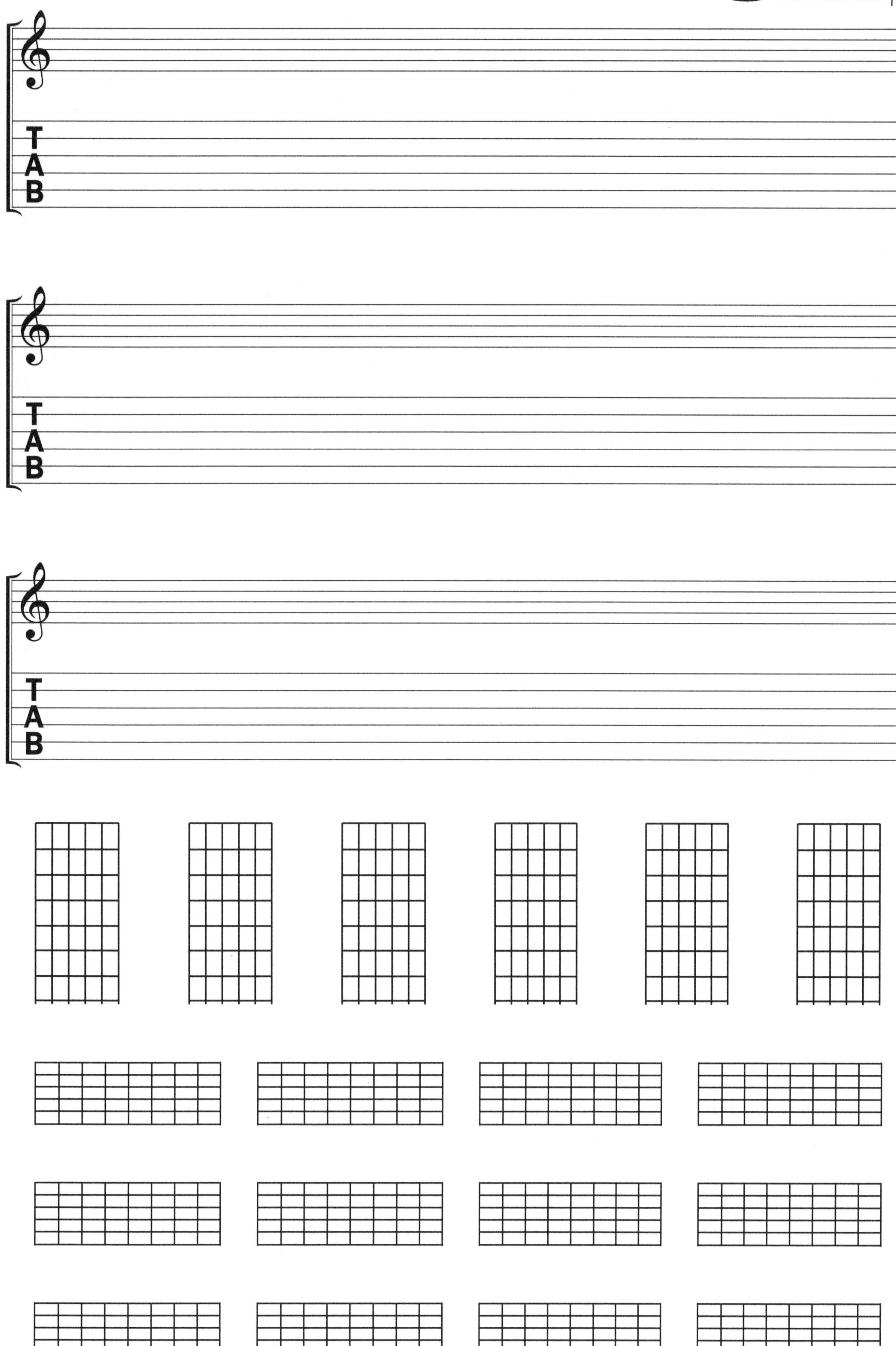

PRACTICE PLANNER

DATE:	METHOD BOOK PAGE(s):									
SUBJECT	**DESCRIPTION / GOALS**	**BPM**	Su	M	T	W	Th	F	Sa
__________ MINUTES										
__________ MINUTES										
__________ MINUTES										
__________ MINUTES										
__________ MINUTES										
__________ MINUTES										
__________ MINUTES										
TOTAL __________ MINUTES										

Teacher Notes

Student Notes

PRACTICE PLANNER

DATE:	METHOD BOOK PAGE(s):								
SUBJECT	**DESCRIPTION / GOALS**	BPM	Su	M	T	W	Th	F	Sa
_______ MINUTES									
_______ MINUTES									
_______ MINUTES									
_______ MINUTES									
_______ MINUTES									
_______ MINUTES									
_______ MINUTES									
TOTAL _______ MINUTES									

Teacher Notes

Student Notes

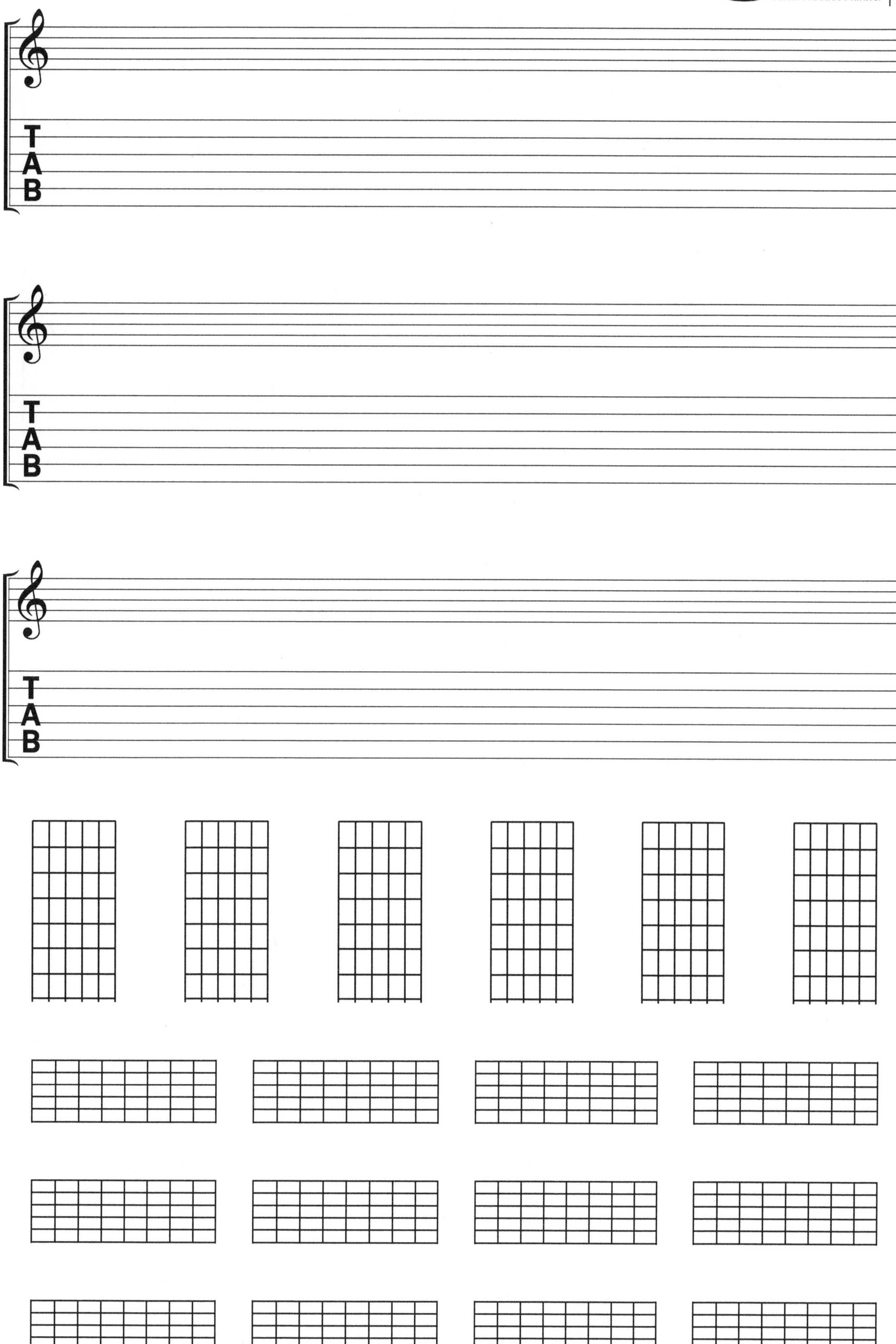

PRACTICE PLANNER

DATE:	METHOD BOOK PAGE(s):									
SUBJECT	**DESCRIPTION / GOALS**	**BPM**	**Su**	**M**	**T**	**W**	**Th**	**F**	**Sa**	
________ MINUTES										
________ MINUTES										
________ MINUTES										
________ MINUTES										
________ MINUTES										
________ MINUTES										
________ MINUTES										
TOTAL ________ **MINUTES**										

Teacher Notes

Student Notes

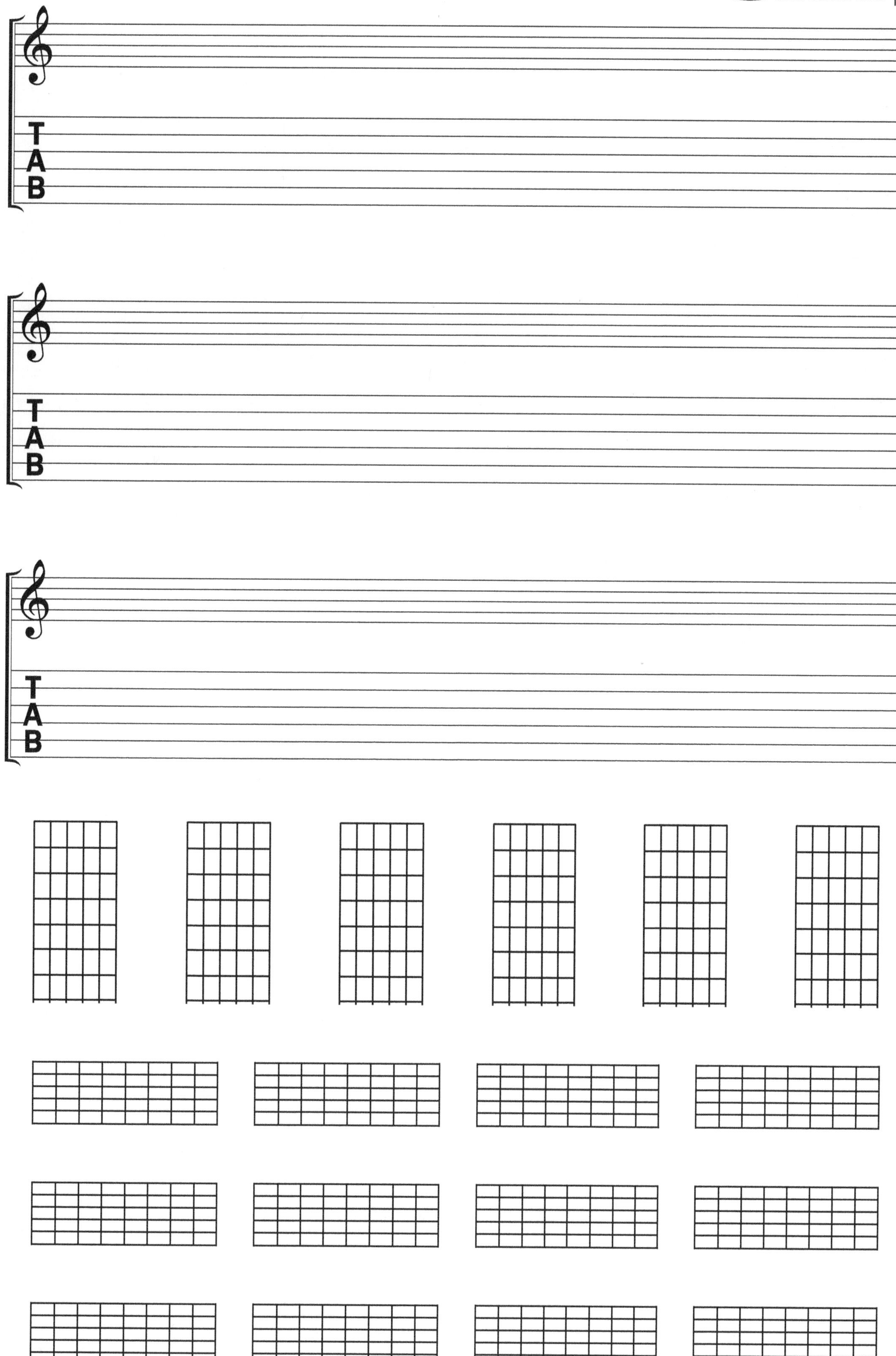

PRACTICE PLANNER

DATE:	METHOD BOOK PAGE(s):								
SUBJECT	**DESCRIPTION / GOALS**	BPM	Su	M	T	W	Th	F	Sa
_______ MINUTES									
_______ MINUTES									
_______ MINUTES									
_______ MINUTES									
_______ MINUTES									
_______ MINUTES									
_______ MINUTES									
TOTAL _______ **MINUTES**									

Teacher Notes

Student Notes

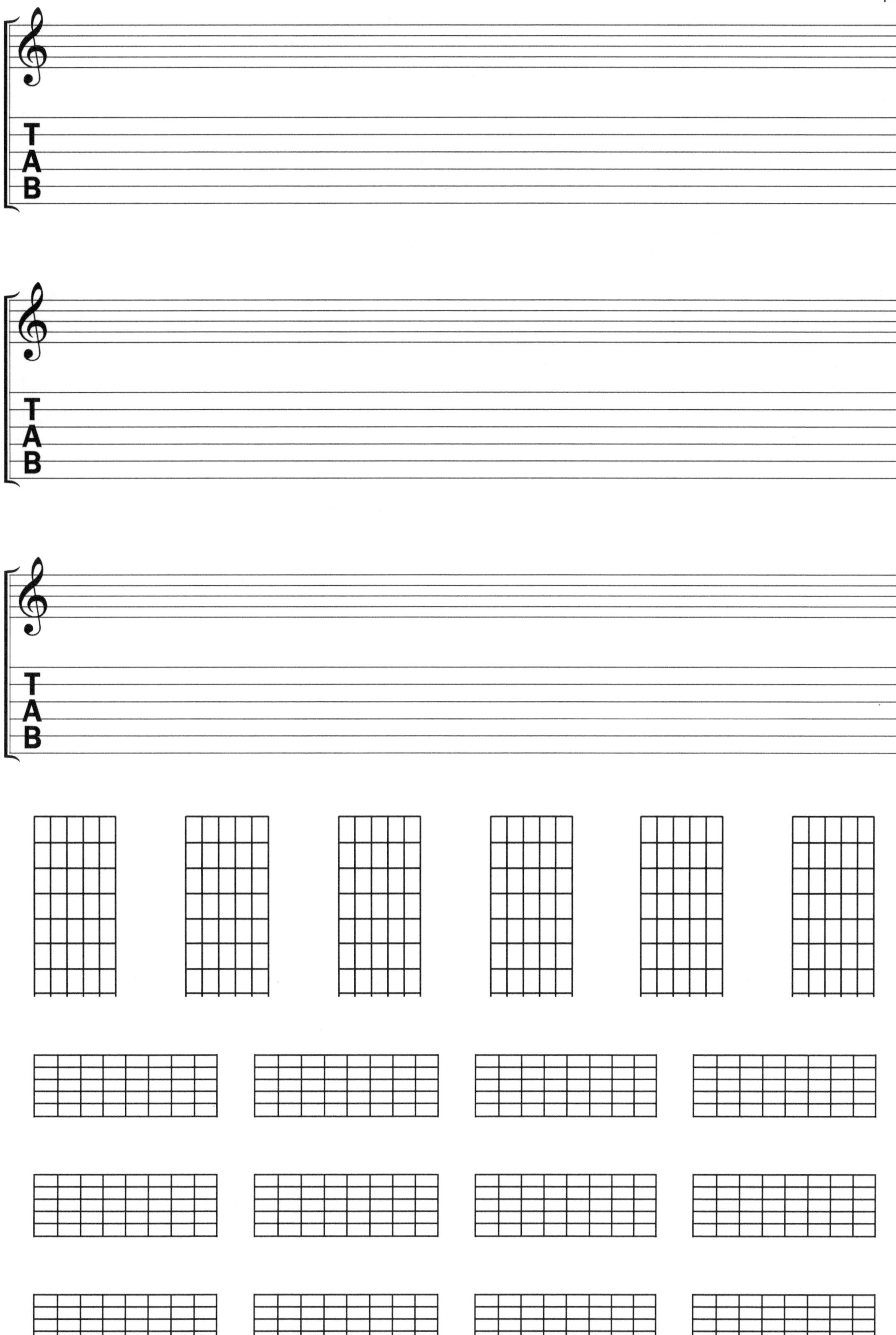

PRACTICE PLANNER

DATE:	METHOD BOOK PAGE(s):								
SUBJECT	DESCRIPTION / GOALS	BPM	Su	M	T	W	Th	F	Sa
_______ MINUTES									
_______ MINUTES									
_______ MINUTES									
_______ MINUTES									
_______ MINUTES									
_______ MINUTES									
_______ MINUTES									
TOTAL _______ MINUTES									

Teacher Notes

Student Notes

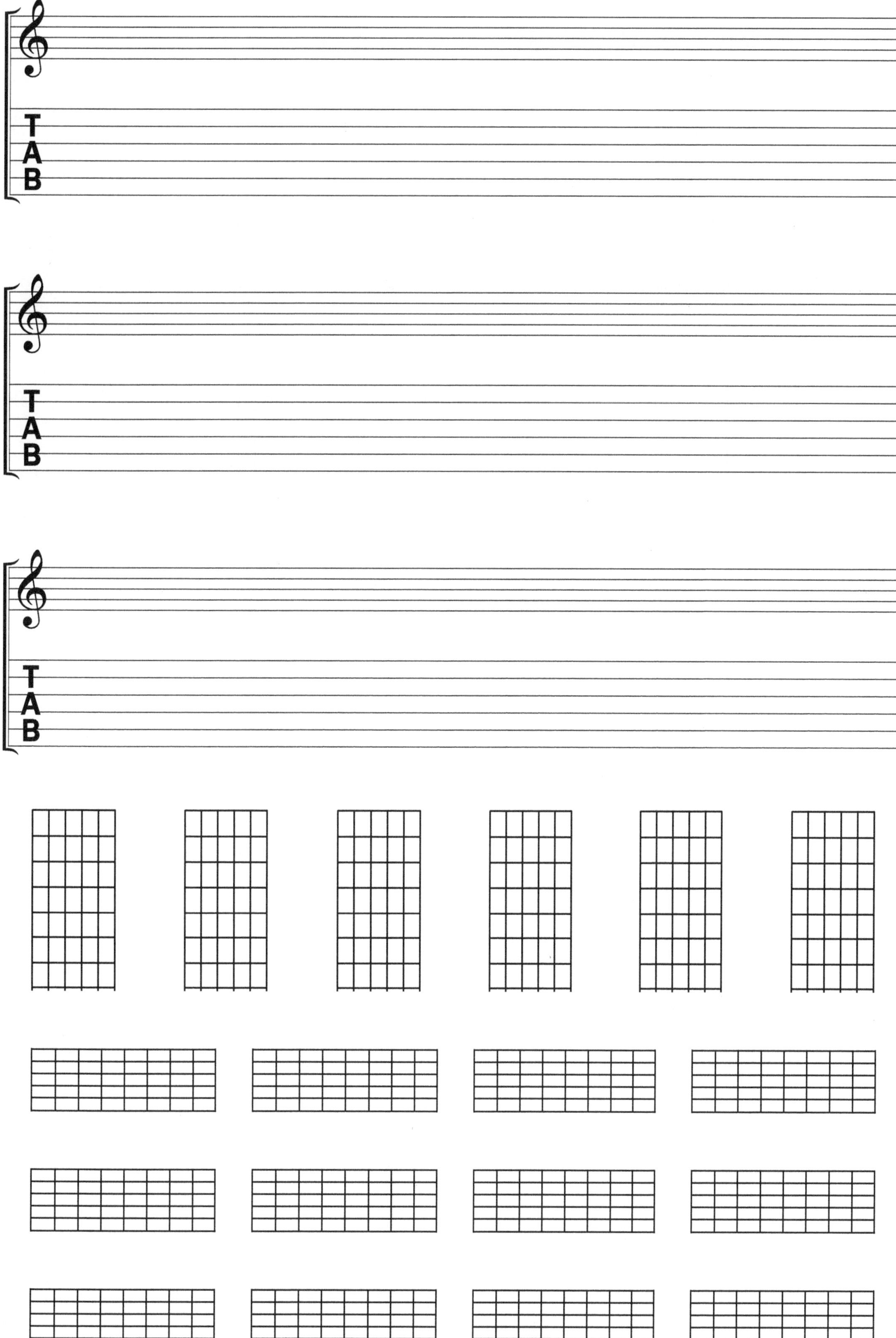

MORE BLANK CHORD AND SCALE FRAMES

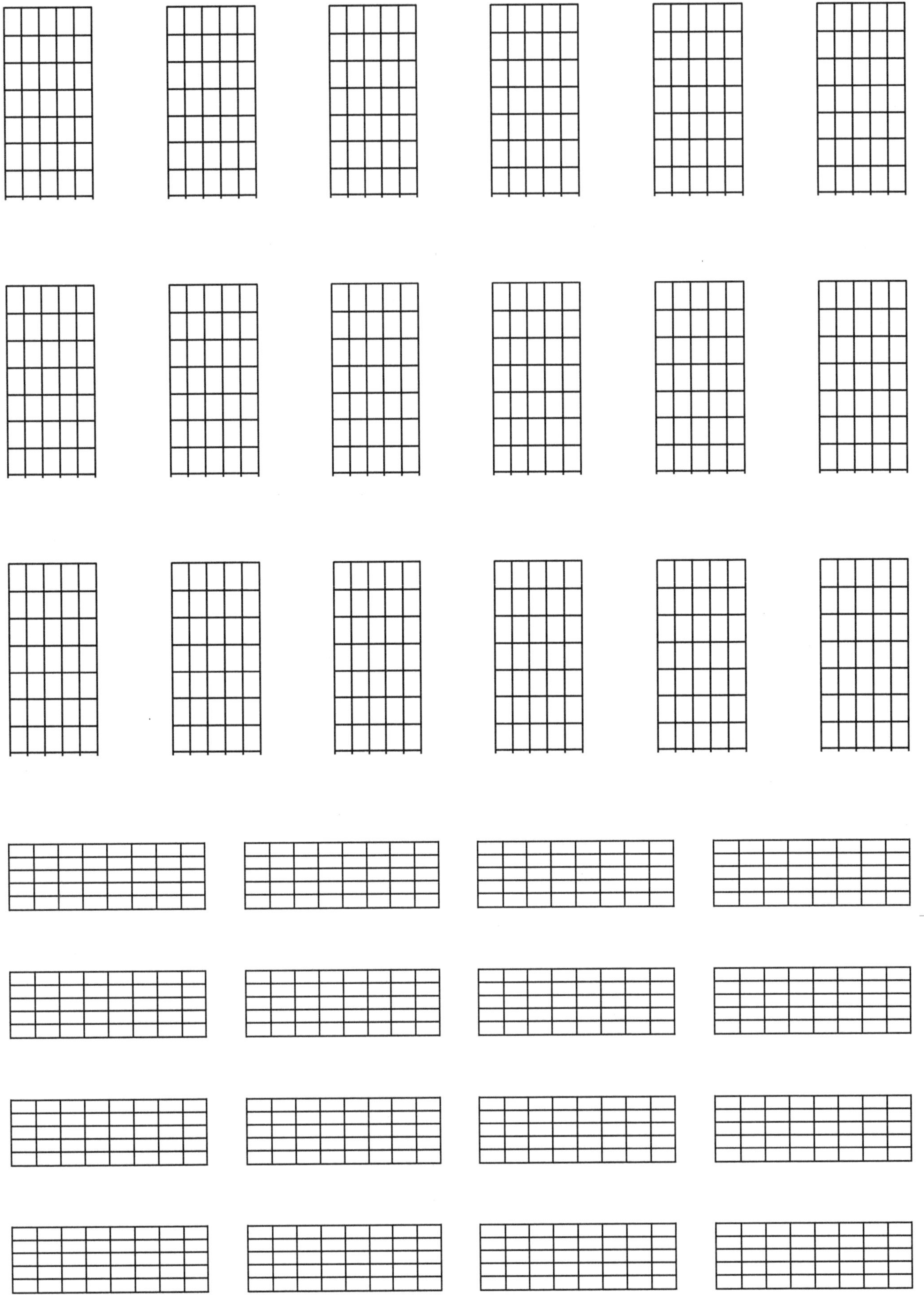